THE
PRAYERS
THAT SECURE
HEAVENLY
ANSWERS

PASTOR ANIETIE AFFIAH

authorHOUSE®

AuthorHouse™
1663 Liberty Drive
Bloomington, IN 47403
www.authorhouse.com
Phone: 833-262-8899

Published by AuthorHouse 09/21/2022

ISBN: 978-1-6655-7031-2 (sc)
ISBN: 978-1-6655-7030-5 (e)

Print information available on the last page.

Any people depicted in stock imagery provided by Getty Images are models,
and such images are being used for illustrative purposes only.
Certain stock imagery © Getty Images.

Scripture quotations marked KJV are from the Holy Bible, King James Version
(Authorized Version). First published in 1611. Quoted from the KJV Classic
Reference Bible, Copyright © 1983 by The Zondervan Corporation.

New King James Version (NKJV) Scripture taken from the New King James Version®.
Copyright © 1982 by Thomas Nelson. Used by permission. All rights reserved

Amplified Bible, Classic Edition (AMPC) Copyright © 1954, 1958,
1962, 1964, 1965, 1987 by The Lockman Foundation

1599 Geneva Bible (GNV) Geneva Bible, 1599 Edition. Published by Tolle Lege Press.
All rights reserved. No part of this publication may be reproduced or transmitted in any
form or by any means, electronic or mechanical, without written permission from the
publisher, except in the case of brief quotations in articles, reviews, and broadcasts

New International Version (NIV) Holy Bible, New International Version®, NIV® Copyright
©1973, 1978, 1984, 2011 by Biblica, Inc.® Used by permission. All rights reserved worldwide.

This book is printed on acid-free paper.

CONTENTS

FOREWORD

My beloved pastor has finally completed a very dynamic, instructive, revealing, and inspirational book on the *Prayers that Secure Heavenly Answers*. As I traverse through the pages of this book, many secrets and guidance are unfolded and if one takes great actions, unanswered prayer will be a thing of the past. It is true, there are many books on prayer, but believe me, there is none that addresses the fundamental mishaps in unanswered prayer as this.

I have read many of them, and they all have something good you can glean from them, but as the author puts it, "This book is compiled with the inspiration of the Holy Spirit with both theory and radical experiential knowledge." I was personally so blessed, salivating through the pages and even taking notes for practical application. Over forty years as a Christian, prayer as I see it is the oxygen for living a dynamic Christian life. We live to learn from each other, and my pastor as always has given us a very insightful prayer manual that will secure heavenly answers if we apply the principles laid out on the pages of this great work.

Take time to prayerfully read through this great masterpiece that Pastor Affiah has finally put to birth. I have encouraged him through the gestation period and celebrate with him for a work well done. It was well worth the wait and the grace and anointing of the Lord Jesus was upon him through the process. I can feel and see it through the volume of contents it carries.

You have got to read this book if you desire a result-oriented prayer life. I highly recommend this book not just to read it, but to have it as a guide through your prayer journey experience. Study it, and apply the practical, well-laid methods for a transforming prayer-answered experience.

Dr. Ephraim J. Udofia, Presiding Bishop
Living Faith Apostolic Ministries
Author of twelve life-transforming books
Raleigh, NC.

DEDICATION

This book is dedicated first to the Lord Jesus Christ – the head of Principalities and Powers, the King of all kings, the Lord of lords, the First and the Last, the Alpha and the Omega, the Beginning, and the Ending.

Second, to my wonderful wife Pastor Colette Affiah who has been a very strong support for me in life, marriage, and ministry. She has stood faithfully by me for many years and is my inspiration in the cause of writing this book. My go to person when I am tired, you are indeed blessed. Thanks for being a wonderful gift to me from God.

Third, to my children. Dr. Emem Johnson, Elijah, Aniekan, Sarah, Jeremiah, Rebecca, and my son-in-law, Mr. Jeremiah Johnson Etuk. Your love and the remembrance of your presence in my life is endearing and inspiring. It has helped me to appreciate how much God has blessed me. Thank you.

Fourth, the church Faith in Christ Church Worldwide (FICCW), is full of spectacular, committed, loving, and caring people. I truly appreciate all of you so much for your warmth of fellowship and contributions to my ministry. Lastly, to the outstanding church leaders in our community, nation, and beyond. May God bless and prosper you and your ministries in Jesus name.

ACKNOWLEDGEMENTS

I would like to express my profound and unreserved gratitude to Bishop Ephraim Udofia who is one of the sources of this book, a man who loves the Lord and desires to see others moving forward.

Let me also acknowledge Pastor Taiwo Ayeni who has contributed in many ways, including thoughts, illustrations, and editing of this book. I also thank Dr. Obi and Pastor Helen Emeh for their contributions.

In addition, I would like to acknowledge my indebtedness and appreciation to many who have helped to make this book a reality: Elder Chris Eze, Elder James Sibenge, and Mother Verital Robert the dedicated group of men and women in Faith in Christ Church Worldwide (FICCW), who fervently prayed ceaselessly for divine wisdom while compiling this book.

I also want to express my gratitude to sister Ngozi Eze for not only being supportive of the project but being steadfast and immovable from its inception. Many thanks are due also to FICCW Church Secretary, Brother Edward Etim, who helped in the printing of the review of the last edited version of this book. Let me also acknowledge the contributions of Magdalene Qua, and Gladys Donkeng in the Media Unit.

My prayer is that the LORD, whose ways are unknown to mortal men, who on many occasions and diverse manners spoke to the heroes of our faith through the prophets and in these last days has spoken to us through His Son Jesus Christ, may speak into your lives for abundant blessings in Jesus name. Amen.

Additionally, I deliver these materials to you with prayers, that the purpose for which God empowered me to compile the book together for the body of Christ will fully be achieved for those who spend time studying it. He will use the revelations that are on every page of this book and the potency of His word to speak healings and deliverances to the downtrodden in Jesus name. Amen.

INTRODUCTION

There are many books written on prayer from a theoretical perspective without any experiential knowledge backing it. This book is compiled with the inspiration of the Holy Spirit with both theory and practical experiential knowledge. Experiential knowledge is required as a strong basis for walking and collaborating with God. We are commanded to run the race with patience and in patience possess our souls. Without patiently learning at the foot of Christ in word and prayer one cannot go far in the race. The Bible encourages us to,

"Call unto me, and I will answer thee, and shew thee great and mighty things, which thou knowest not." (Jer. 33:3 KJV).

That is the benefit of seeking the face of the Lord in prayer. The inspiring promise here is that He will show you great and mighty things you have never known before. That should be a great motivating factor to pray or diligently seek Him.

For example, in my few years of ministry, I have seen the Lord do miraculous things such as blind eyes popping open, fibroids melting away, kidney stones flushed out, sickle cell anemia blood type turning to AA, and bone cancer healed, as well as broken marriages restored through the power of prayers.

This book *The Prayers That Secure Heavenly Answers* is based on scriptural godly wisdom, inspired by the Holy Spirit, and borne out of practical and firsthand experiences. I want to assure you that the paradigm used in this book, if applied very well, will revolutionize, energize, and change your mind-set on prayer. You will surely experience how quickly God answers prayers. I am excited and bubbling in my spirit to present to you this mystery which none of *"..the princes of this world,.."* knew. (I Cor. 2:6 KJV)

Except you gain access to biblical insights, your prayer life will remain stagnant. This wisdom is from above and glory be to God that it has been revealed to us. The Lord, Jesus made it explicitly clear in Mark 4:11 KJV that "..***Unto you it is given to know the mystery of the kingdom of God:...***"

Friends your prayers are not meant to take long, but there are always conflicts between holy and unholy angels, in serious spiritual encounters. Hence, to get our prayers answered, we must do all we can to resist them by standing our ground as we read in the book of Daniel 10:12-13 KJV.

"*...for from the first day that didst set thine heart to understand, and to chasten thyself before thy God, thy words were heard, and I am come for thy words. But the prince of the kingdom of Persia withstood me one and twenty days:...*" (Dan. 10:12-13 KJV).

The question is how do we deal with these conflicts without the power of prayer? How do we get our prayers answered without any delay? To get these and many other questions answered, I will identify seven key strategies, and techniques that will deliver your answer to your doorsteps without delay.

The cause of the delay is the fact that you did not use the appropriate keys, just as in the natural if you do not use the right key to your door, or car, you cannot gain access, unless you break it. No wonder Apostle James says:

"***Ye ask, and receive not, because ye ask amiss,...***" (Jas 4:3 KJV).

Welcome to your direct call to heaven and to the prayers that secure the quickest answer and turn things around in your life. However, before you turn to Chapter One of this book, pray this prayer with me:

"*Father God, I believe your word is quick, powerful, and sharper than any two-edged sword. Let your word travel on my behalf to every dark house, or prison where the enemy locks up my destiny. Let your word move like fire and hammer that break the rocky places and take me out of satanic imprisonment in Jesus' name Amen.*"

CHAPTER ONE

WHAT IS PRAYER?

"And all things, whatsoever ye shall ask in prayer, believing, ye shall receive." (Matt 21:22 KJV)

Prayer is a spiritual communication platform, a process that allows one to talk and listen to God, while having an intimate fellowship with Him. It is a vehicle, so-to-speak, of conveying your message across to God and receiving answers from Him. Real prayers begin with an intimate relationship with God based on having continuous fellowship with Him. It is not just enough to know Him through having a relationship with Him, it is important as well to service that relationship through daily quiet time and fellowship with Him in prayer and worship!

A good example of intimacy in prayer is found in the prayer of Solomon to God in 1 Kings 8:25-26 KJV

"Therefore now, LORD God of Israel, keep with thy servant David my father that thou promisedst him, saying, There shall not fail thee a man in my sight to sit on the throne of Israel; so that thy children take heed to their way, that they walk before me as thou hast walked before me. And now, O God of Israel, let thy word, I pray thee, be verified, which thou spakest unto thy servant David my father."

The prayer of Solomon here reveals a man who had walked intimately with God. Even his choice of words and knowledge of the subject shows that he intimately knew God. He understood the fact that God is the only way out and he placed his fate in His hands.

Solomon also demonstrated faith in God, believing He could do what He had promised, and he went ahead to seek His face for the promises! Just like Solomon, for us to make an impact in our prayers with God our faith must be based on exercising our belief in His word. The Lord Jesus confirmed this to us in Matthew 21:22 that we receive whatsoever we ask in prayer, if we believe.

Prayer is the believer's source of strength and peace. It is a channel of grace, and a medium of joy through which we open our hearts to the One who created the universe by the power of His word. It is a weapon given to us to go through and break through the strongholds of the power of darkness. The direct dialogue or conversation we have with God unleashes His supernatural power that takes over our battle and brings us into our glorious destiny.

Prayer is also a desperate cry for the heavenly answer *"...and the prophet Isaiah the son of Amoz, prayed and cried to heaven."* (2 Chron. 32:20 KJV). When you lift your eyes up towards the hills of the Lord, you are assured in your spirit that your help is coming from the Lord - the one who made heaven and earth. (Ps. 121:1-2).

Prayer opens the channel of God's divine plans in our lives. This conduit gives us access that guarantees total victory as James 5:13 encourages us to do: *"Is any among you afflicted? Let him pray...."*

It is like a vehicle which is used to transport various products to their desired destinations. The Psalmist declares:

"Blessed be the LORD, who bears our burden day by day, The God who is our salvation!" (Ps. 68:19 AMP).

Please understand that your prayers as believers are like golden bowls full of incense, fragrant spice, and gums for burning.

"And another angel came and stood at the altar, having a golden censer; and there was given unto him much incense, that he should offer it with the prayers of all saints upon the golden altar which was before the throne." (Rev 8:3 KJV)

It is one of the greatest tools one can use to fight the unseen battles of life when it is offered in reverence and godly fear. The prayer that secures heavenly answers must be offered with a broken heart and contrite spirit. The word prayer is specifically used by King David as he cried to God for help:

"Hear me when I call, O God of my righteousness: Thou hast enlarged me when I was in distress; Have mercy upon me and hear my prayer." (Ps. 4:1 KJV).

Furthermore, in Psalms 17:1-2 KJV he categorically made his case with God, and clearly stated his desires or expectations from Him:

"Hear the right, O LORD, attend unto my cry, Give ear unto my prayer, which goeth not out of feigned lips. Let my sentence come forth from thy presence; Let thine eyes behold the things that are equal."

Breaking this down briefly, he asked God not to be deaf to his weeping, but to take heed to the turmoil and pain His servant was going through. He used these words in his plea to God to hear his prayer, and to know that it did not come from deceitful lips.

Prayer is that solemn moment that you pour out your heart in an intimate dialogue with your creator, the one who promised never to leave you, nor forsake you (Heb 13:5 KJV). At this point in intimate prayer, you are establishing that connection within your mind and heart, while giving yourself the opportunity to have a deeper experience with the source of your life. The one who is consistently inviting you to call upon Him in the time of trouble, He will deliver you and you will glorify Him (Jer. 33:3 KJV).

The scripture above refers to a direct call that has neither interference nor disruption, and once you choose to make this call it means that you are opting to step aside from the natural realm to the supernatural. The word "call" means to properly address someone by name, to declare, to summon e.g., to invite a famous guest to an occasion. God's invitation is always out there for those who are willing and obedient.

Earlier in this book, we saw Him making the same call in Jeremiah 33 verse 3. Prayer is the biggest spiritual investment you can ever make in life. In case you are wondering what an investment is? It is putting money into a business or project with the hope of making a profit or return, which businesspeople refer to as Return on Investment (ROI). When we invest our resources, or time to seek the face of God in prayer our spiritual blessings will keep on increasing more and more. The true secret of prayer is that its gains come through perseverance, patience, and unwavering endurance. "*By your steadfastness and patient endurance, you shall win the true life of your souls.*" (Lk. 21:19 AMPC).

It is important to know that even though, God cares deeply about our problems, He is waiting for us to bring them to Him in prayer. When a heavy load is taken away from a person, he gains speed.

Understand that while he had the load on him, every step he takes diminishes his strength, and this slows him down. He is weighed down by this burden, but when his thought or intent is conceived in prayer and poured out to our heavenly Father in intimate but thoughtful cry, He steps in immediately to bear the burden for him with signs and wonders following.

We commune with the Omniscient (All Knowing) God, as the Bible confirms in Psalms 139:2-4 KJV:

"*Thou knowest my down sitting and mine uprising, thou understandest my thought afar off. Thou compassest my path and my lying down, and art acquainted with all my ways. For there is not a word in my tongue, But, lo, O LORD, thou knowest it altogether.*"

When a thought is conceived in your heart, and you direct it to the All-Knowing God in faith, the One who knows your movements, paths, and ways, your thoughts shall be established.

Everyone that believes in the name of Jesus must use this tool. It is one of the weapons that forces every closed door to open, gives birth to our dreams and releases our destiny. In Acts 12:5 KJV we read:

"*Peter therefore was kept in prison: but prayer was made without ceasing of the church unto God for him.*"

In this passage, we are told that Peter was locked up in prison, but believers who not only understood the power of prayer but comprehended the prayer that could provoke heaven to answer, made a desperate cry to God. They prayed the prayer that secures heavenly answers and touches the heart of God. Our God who never slumbers and ceases to be watchful answered their cry. It is His plan that His children must always be safe. Therefore, in His loving kindness God moved the same night that they prayed *"..when Herod would have brought him forth,..."* (Acts 12:6 KJV)

That same night, even though Peter was sleeping, yet suddenly the supernatural power of God showed up. While Herod was still rejoicing over his catch, and hoping to execute judgment the next day, God mobilized the hosts of heaven to open the prison doors. Imagine a prison door opening on its own accord, without human intervention! This could only be God at work.

It was not like they had the type of technology we have today where gates or doors could be opened remotely. For example, if you go to big grocery stores like Wal-Mart, Food Lion, Shop Rite, City Mall and many others, the doors will open on their own accord just by sensing your presence. But this was not the case with Peter, heaven intervened to forcefully open the prison doors.

The miraculous release of Peter continues as we read in Acts 12:9-10 KJV, and to him it was like a dream too good to be true:

"And he went out, and followed him; and wist not that it was true which was done by the angel; but thought he saw a vision. When they were past the first and second ward, they came unto the iron gate that leadeth unto the city; which opened to them of his own accord: and they went out, and passed on through one street: and forthwith the angel departed from him."

This account was a direct manifestation of divine power. In this case, the soldiers stationed at intervals at the entrance of the prison, were all knocked out by divine Valium pills that made them fall asleep like babies while Peter was being set free by an angel. When the supernatural power erupted, the iron gate of the prison and the city gate that secured the city gave way. The presence of God's messenger caused the door of the prisons to be opened. Both Peter and the host of heaven who were on divine errand silently passed through, while deep sleep fell on the soldiers which easily facilitated Peter's escape. God is great!

CHAPTER TWO

PRAYING THE
WORD OF GOD

"Is not my word like as a fire? saith the LORD; and like a hammer that breaketh the rock in pieces?" (Jer. 23:29 KJV)

A. Power in the Word.

The word of God is so potent that we must review the various dimensions of the word, its potential and necessity in the place of prayer. The understanding of these should help us to appropriately deploy the word effectively at targeted sources. For example, using the word as a sword to attack either a wall or other physical barriers is foolish and ignorant. The appropriate weapon to use in this instance is the hammer. You use the word as a hammer to break down walls and the word as a fire to burn down an evil force or fortress. The various forms or manifestations of the word are itemized below for your review. Be blessed as you wisely go through them with a willing heart and thereafter be equipped for spiritual warfare!

1. The Word is a consuming Fire!

The word of God expectedly is a burning fire or what else should it be if God Himself is a consuming fire (Heb 12:29 KJV)? The fire of God's word is so potent that even the forces of darkness could not withstand it. The principalities and powers, and other demonic forces clear off the way because of the potent heat emanating from the word. Also, sickness and diseases give way to the victory of the fire of word uncontested.

When Jeremiah released the word, it shook the foundation of powers and brought solutions to protracted problems. Many who were under the bondage of slavery got their deliverance. You too as a believer can deploy the fire of God's word to consume the fortress of the enemy. This is because, as mentioned earlier your Father, who is God, is Himself a consuming fire (Heb 12:29 KJV)! Therefore, empower yourself through meditation on the word, be fueled by the word of God and become a fire carrier in Jesus' name. It is well.

2. The Word is a Hammer

Beyond the word being a burning fire, Jeremiah makes us to understand that it is also a hammer that breaks the rocks into pieces. The word of God is so potent that it breaks satanic barricades. The walls of Jericho fell when the children of God shouted after the sound of trumpets that were blown the seventh time (Josh 6:16, 20 KJV). When the walls fell it was as if the angels in heaven used hammers to break them down. This reminds us again of the words of Jeremiah that God's word is both like a fire and a hammer that breaks the rock in pieces (Jer. 23:29 KJV):

The hammer of God's word smashes the walls of satanic resistance and breaks them to pieces. But you must know how to wield this hammer. You must have a depth of the bank of God's word to know which word to deploy in prayer warfare. It is not just about throwing words but releasing targeted potent scriptures to destroy evil foundations!

It is imperative to know that when a mighty man lifts a sledgehammer and brings it down with great force on the stone that he wants to break, that stone has no chance of survival - it *"..shall be broken in pieces.".* (Is 8:9 KJV) The word of God can create something that was not in existence to come into being, and it is evident that the power in the word causes supernatural phenomenon to occur. This is evident in Psalms 33:6, and 9 KJV where we read that:

"By the word of the LORD were the heavens made; And all the host of them by the breath of his mouth.

For he spake, and it was done; He commanded, and it stood fast."

The devil is not comfortable with the word of God which is *"...a hammer that breaketh the rock in pieces."* For this reason, he does all he can to keep believers away from the word and deceives them by making them to engage in wordless but fruitless prayer. Without engaging the word, you are like a lawyer in court without a prepared brief, but only ready to just focus on generalities! Beloved, the Lord insists *"Produce your cause, saith the LORD; bring forth your strong reasons, saith the King of Jacob."* (Is. 41:21 KJV). This is not a suggestion but a command!

Picking up the issue of the hammer again, to effectively use one, I will suggest that you consider learning to use a sledgehammer to have a true picture of this subject. For example, before somebody can use a hammer very well, he must be skilled enough to swing it in such a way that he does not lose his balance. He also must have the stamina to stand his ground as he continuously hit the object hard until it is broken to pieces.

The goal of using a hammer is to strike an object with it. And any person who is trying to break a pile of rocks, only must hit them as hard as he can, and keep hitting until they are all broken to pieces. Brethren, if you are tormented with any form of infirmity: cancer, heart disease, kidney failure, diabetes and other stubborn diseases that refuse to go, it is time to use your hammer. You must lift the hammer of the word in prayer to strike and continue to hit the enemy until they are completely broken. Brethren, it is necessary to *"Pray without ceasing."* (1 Thess. 5:17 KJV)

When you use the hammer of the word of God as commanded by God the result will be amazing and wonderful. If there are agents of the devil ridiculing your lives, continue to strike them with the hammer of the word of God until they are broken to pieces. The word of God in Isaiah 8:9 KJV has already promised us victory if we do so:

"Associate yourselves, O ye people, and ye shall be broken in pieces; and give ear, all ye of far countries: gird yourselves, and ye shall be broken in pieces; gird yourselves, and ye shall be broken in pieces."

Use the word to hit the rocks, barriers, and obstacles until they are broken to pieces. Remember that every hit on an object commences the process of disintegration or fragmentation and therefore continue to use the hammer of the word without ceasing until you achieve your goal. You may be going through some spiritual attacks at night or be physically tormented with diverse kind of infirmities in your body; just continue praying the word of God to address the matter. Pray the word of God in faith without ceasing and wait to see God move against your enemies!

3. The word is a Sword

"For the word of God is quick, and powerful, and shaper than any twoedged sword, piercing even to the diving asunder of soul and spirit, and of the joints and marrow, and is a discerner of the thoughts and intents of the heart." (Heb. 4:12 KJV)

The inspired and infallible word of God is the most powerful, and active weapon that has ever been known and used on the planet earth. And as the scripture confirms, it is *"… shaper than any twoedged sword "* Its validity and potency is neither unquestionable nor un-deniable and it never fails to deliver! Its values are the same everywhere and anywhere you use it in the world. You can use it to pay for your health, ransom your family and deploy it as pleasant words that *"are as an honeycomb, sweet to the soul, and health to the bones. "* (Prov. 16:24 KJV).

The word has mysterious binding authority. For instance, when

Isaac discovered that he had been deceived and had wrongly blessed Jacob instead of Esau as intended, he declared: "*..and I have eaten of all before thou camest, and have blessed him? yea, and he shall be blessed.*" (Gen 27:33 KJV).

He said the blessing had been given to Jacob; he would be blessed and there is nothing I could do to reverse it. That concluded the whole matter.

4.   The word is an Arrow

The word of God is also like an arrow that once it is shot, it cannot be recalled. We can see the irresistible force and the creative power it carries as described in Isaiah 55:11 KJV:

"So shall my word be that goeth forth out of my mouth: it shall not return unto me void, but it shall accomplish that which I please, and it shall prosper in the thing whereto I sent it."

If you want a quick answer to your prayers, you must learn to pray the word of God effectively. You must use the arrows of the word to pierce the hearts of the enemy. Deploy the arrows of the word to kill the enemies of your souls. Suffer not a witch to live – Be wise!

B. Word Declaration:

Beloved, please make these prophetic declarations below in faith:

Father, according to your word in 1 Chronicles 16:33 KJV, you commanded the trees of the wood to sing at your presence; Lazarus was forced out of the grave to proof your power; impotent folks celebrated their release at the pool Bethesda because of the irrefutable power of your presence, and signs and wonders took place at the valley of dry bones. Let heaven release supernatural breakthroughs for me in Jesus' name (John 5:1 and Ezekiel 36:1-11 KJV).

Father, in the name of Jesus, I declare that the power of your word will break every obstacle and replace it with miracles. I command every arrow of the wicked against my health, family, career, and business to return to the sender in Jesus' name (Psalms 76:3 KJV).

*Father in the name of Jesus, I declare according to your word, that "...... **affliction shall not rise up second time.**" (Nahum 1:9 KJV). Therefore, any pattern of darkness that the enemy has designed against my health shall be destroyed in Jesus' name. "**And it shall come to pass in that day, that his burden shall be taken away from off thy shoulder, and his yoke from off thy neck and the yoke shall be destroyed because of the anointing.**" (Is. 10:27 KJV).*

*I declare every marital spell, enchantment, delay, failure, and frustration be broken in Jesus' name. Father in the name of Jesus; let the rain of divine favor drop down from above, and let the clouds pour down righteousness. Let the earth open on my behalf so that my salvation will bear fruit. Clear away financial emptiness from my hands as it is written, "**And the Lord gave the people favor in the sight of the Egyptians, so that they lent unto them such things as they required. And they spoiled the Egyptians.**" (Ex. 12:36 KJV)*

C. The Priority of the Word

The word of God is often personified as an instrument for the execution of God's plans on earth for instance, the Bible says:

"**He sendeth forth his commandment upon earth: His word runneth very swiftly.**

He sendeth out his word, and melteth them: He causeth his wind to blow, and the waters flow." (Ps. 147:15,18 KJV).

If you want to experience His divine plans in your life, consider His word as a priority in your daily prayers. In most cases we pray and repeat words over and over making it redundant and without substance. His words deliver your prayer to heaven and never returns to you void (Is. 55:11 KJV).

God is reaching out to men who will return to God's established word saying. "**.... we will give ourselves continually to prayer, and to** *the ministry of the word*" (Acts 6:4 KJV). Every problem has a specific solution in the word of God; therefore, every believer must go for it.

D. Why does the word carry so much power?

The word is God himself *"and the Word was God"* (Jn. 1:1 KJV) *"...and His name is called The Word of God"* (Rev. 19:13 KJV). The scripture tells us that the word was God and dwells with God in the beginning. Without any doubt, this means that God and His Word are one. God's word is an invisible power that resides in Him. It is a spiritual force that when it is released, it turns the natural into the supernatural

God breathed His spirit into a molded clay, and the invisible word turn dust into human. In the same instance, every component of the body needed to make it work effectively like the heart, brain, eyes, nose, ears, tongue, muscles, lungs, and intestine etc. began to function in the "dust" as human "....*and man became a living soul.*" (Gen. 2:7 KJV).

The word is a spiritual password that gives you access to whatever you believe God for. When you declare His word in prayer it guarantees that your expectation would be met, and it speeds up the answers to your prayers as well. Praying the word of God is the most effective and quickest way to get an answer to your prayers. His word has a direct connection between the degree to which our minds are shaped by the scripture and the answer to our prayers. The Bible in John 15:7 KJV affirms this position below:

"If ye abide in me, and my words abide in you, ye shall ask what ye will, and it shall be done unto you."

If you take time to review the Acts of the Apostles, you will notice that the apostles made it a point of duty to pray the scriptures and not their own words always! In Acts 4:24-25, 29, 31 KJV we see a good example of their pattern of praying.

"And when they heard that, they lifted up their voice to God with one accord, and said, Lord, thou art God, which hast made heaven, and earth, and the sea, and all that in them is:

Who by the mouth of thy servant David hast said, why did the heathen rage, and the people imagine vain things?

And now, Lord, behold their threatening: and grant unto thy servants, that with all boldness they may speak thy word,

And when they had prayed, the place was shaken where they were assembled together; and they were all filled with Holy Ghost and they spake the word of God with boldness."

Our Lord only deals with petitions that His Son Jesus Christ has had His hand in formulating. He is the guarantor of every answer to our prayer as it is revealed in 1 John 5:14 that: *"..if we ask anything according to His will, he hears us."* (1 Jn. 5:14 NKJV)

E. What is in the Word of God?

The Word of God is the spirit of God.

"It is the spirit that quickeneth: the flesh profiteth nothing: the words that I speak unto you, they are spirit, and they are life." (Jn. 6:63 KJV).

His word is the spirit because He is the Word, and the spirit of God dwells in Him (John 1:1 KJV). What is in the word of God? Life is in the Word, because *"In him was life; and the life was the light of men. And the light shineth in darkness; and the darkness comprehended it not."* (Jn. 1:4-5 KJV). In addition, *"... in him we live, and move, and have our being;...."* (Acts 17:28 KJV). There is no argument that our life is in Him, and in Him we live.

The word of God is what God speaks, whether it is about His promise, or addressing a life-threatening situation; whether it is in the law or gospel, they are revealed to His children.

The truth is that the word of God is capable of detecting, exposing, or bringing to light every hidden agenda that the devil must have launched in the dark. The word is powerful whether preached, read, or communicated by conversation, meditation, or a deep impression on the heart filled with the Holy Spirit. Its virtue is inexplicable, and it has the power to change your life forever (1Kings 17:24 KJV). The word is a penetrating sword that goes deeper into joint bones and marrow (Heb. 4:12 KJV). Understand that God is not a "wishy-washy' God will help you a great deal. He said what He meant, and He means exactly what He says. He works through the instrumentality of His word.

"*Not a word failed of any good thing which the LORD had spoken to the house of Israel. All came to pass.*" (Josh. 21:45 NKJV).

The incomparable word of God is a life force, it is neither lifeless, nor powerless but able to produce effect. Scientific study shows that the medical scanner can have a close look inside the body. One of the scientific papers reviewed states and I quote that "The powerful magnetic device called Nuclear Magnetic resonance scanner can help doctors to see inside joints, cartilage, ligament etc. for detecting various spots in the human body." (Tanya Lewis published August 2017).

If technology can pinpoint or expose what is hidden in the human system, how much more the sure word which was established in Christ with a covenant which is based upon the shed blood of Jesus Christ.

"*For the Word that God speaks is alive and full of power [making it active, operative, energizing, and effective]; it is sharper than any two-edged sword, penetrating to the dividing line of the breath of life (soul) and [the immoral] spirit, and of joints and marrow [of the deepest parts of our nature], exposing and sifting and analyzing and judging the very thoughts and purposes of the heart.*" (Heb 4:12 AMPC).

The word of God has the power to devour that which God has not planted. The piercing or the penetrating power of God's word can destroy the enemies of your soul. It is as simple as for you to take hold of the word that addresses that problem or situation, declare it, confess, and meditate on it as you confront sickness in your body. Since the word of God is designed for this purpose, it will move into your joints, bones, and marrow even into the deepest parts of your body, and when it reaches the very center of the problem it proves its power by eliminating the culprit.

F. Healing Scriptures

There are countless scriptures identified in the Bible that believers could use to deal with any situation. From the beginning, God has spoken His words that have powerful influence on the earth. When He said, "...**Let there be light and there was light.**" (Gen. 1:3 NKJV) His words made it possible. God's action here is the evidence of God's word in action. When God speaks things happen and Hebrews 11:3 (NKJV) clearly tells us that:

"**By faith we understand that the worlds were framed by the word of God, so that the things which are seen were not made of things which are visible.**"

We are the image of God, created in His likeness, therefore we carry the power of God as well when we speak. We can release the same power in our word to counter any ugly situation, or infirmity as God assures us that: "**...I am alert and active, watching over My word to perform it.**" (Jer. 1:12 AMPC).

He will perform whatever we decree, declare, or proclaim if we can believe (Mk 11:23 AMPC). God is watching over us, looking, and searching for someone who would use His word to fight the invisible battle. You must realize that the power of God in your tongue will heal you of whatever sickness you might be going through. Some Christians claim sickness. For instance, I heard someone say:

"**I am diabetic, or I have bipolar, or my parents died of heart attack or cancer.**"

And he believes that he will suffer the same fate. The danger here is that the word of God tells us that as a man "**... thinketh in his heart, so is he:..**" (Prov. 23:7 KJV). And more serious is the fact that God profoundly said in Numbers 14:28 that:

"**Say unto them, As truly as I live, saith the LORD, as ye have spoken in mine ears, so will I do to you:**"

So, beloved be warned and watch your mouth! There is power of life and death in your tongue so watch what you say, it may be very costly at the end (Prov. 18:21 KJV).

As a believer saved by grace, you are a new creation in Christ as we read in 2 Corinthians 5:17:

"Therefore if any man be in Christ, he is a new creature: old things are passed away; behold, all things are become new."

Not is only our past behind us when we are saved, born again of the water and of the spirit, but we are renamed as *"new creature"* by the blood of Jesus. You understand you are accepted into His kingdom because you have been washed, sanctified, and purified by the blood of Jesus. Redemption is the way of escape and the receipt of exemption from inherited or generational curses. (Gal. 3:13 KJV).

You are free by God's divine promises from the sins of the fathers. God through Ezekiel asked a profound question in Ezekiel 18:2-3 and gave His verdict on the matter in verse 20 KJV.

"What mean ye, that ye use this proverb concerning the land of Israel, saying, The fathers have eaten sour grapes, and the children's teeth are set on edge? As I live, saith the Lord God, ye shall not have occasion any more to use this Proverb in Israel.

The soul that sinneth, it shall die. The son shall not bear the iniquity of the father,.." (Ezek. 18:2-3, 20 KJV).

Jesus terminated inherited curses and He came to save us from sins to make the bill of our freedom strong on delivery. When you tender in prayer this divine decree from God, it becomes a legal tender because of the blood of Jesus. God does not answer the prayer of sinners (John 9:31). If God answers the prayer of sinners, why then do we see the same manner of death that occurred in your parent's generation happening again to others who have no Christ and could not apply the word in potent prayer?

If what happened to them is happening to you, that will make the word of God to become a lie! Please know that the very day you gave your life to Jesus buried and resurrected with Christ you came out a new man. All the affliction your parents suffered ceased from that moment and you left them at the foot of the cross.

We see God's lovingkindness in John 5:4 where mercy visited people who have long-standing sicknesses. A good case in point is the man who had been there for thirty-eight years, and God sent him help through the visitation of Jesus in verses 5 - 9 of that chapter. The chapter in verse 4 collectively describes the situation thus:

"For an angel went down at a certain season into the pool, and troubled the water: whosoever then first after the troubling of the water stepped in was made whole of whatsoever disease he had." (Jn. 5:4 KJV).

There was " *..a great multitude of impotent folk, of blind, halt, withered,…"* who all gathered around at Bethesda, *"…waiting for the moving of the water"* but could not get their healings (Jn. 5:3 KJV). However, when Jesus arrived and cured the one who had been hopelessly and helplessly bound for thirty-eight years, he left the place completely made whole. Whatever sickness may be in your bloodline was taken away at the time you received Him as your Lord and Savior, and at water baptism you were left with no mark because you are a new creature in Christ Jesus by faith through His blood. The scripture in Proverbs 13:22 (AMPC) tells us: *"A good man leaves an inheritance [of moral stability and goodness] to his children's children,."*

Stop thinking that people who have died in your family have left infirmities such as cancer, heart disease, and kidney failure for you. That is the lie of the devil! According to God's divine mercies they are supposed to leave as inheritance behind for you, moral stability, goodness, and wealth and not sickness. It has come to a time that every prayer you offer must be backed up with the word of God because praying your own word does not accomplish that purpose. The word of God declares:

"So shall my word be that goeth forth out of my mouth: it shall not return unto me void, but it shall accomplish that which I please, and it shall prosper in thing whereto I sent it." (Is. 55:11 KJV)

The tools to destabilize evil plan are not too high for you, it is not far from you, and not confined to intellectuals and Romans 10:8 KJV declares that: "*…The word is nigh thee, even in thy mouth, and in thy heart: that is, the word of faith, which we preach;"*

CHAPTER THREE

PRESENT YOUR CASE IN PRAYER

"Produce your cause, said the LORD; bring forth your strong reasons, said the King of Jacob." (Is. 41:21 KJV).

The basic purpose of prayer is to spread your hopelessness and helplessness before Him who can help you solve your problems. Therefore, as you pray the word of God you must present your strong reasons. For example, if you feel as if you are just alone, facing life-threatening sickness, and going through excruciating pains, while the fear of death comes knocking at your door, it is time to deploy the weapon of God's word in prayer. Also, when you are on your sick bed feeling discouraged, or frustrated in life, and the doors of mercy are shut against you, it is time you begin to declare God's words by stating your strong reasons or cause. *"...Set forth your case, that you may be justified (proved right)."* (Is. 43:26 AMPC)

Because the devil is the accuser of the brethren, you must always produce strong reasons why you want to be justified or show that you are just, and that you are the righteousness of God in Christ Jesus (2 Cor 5:21). You must demonstrate that you were unjustly accused of the crime and therefore punished with undue severity. Your argument should be since you may experience light affliction which is for a moment but

"..the rod of the wicked shall not rest on the lot of the righteous...." (Ps 125:3 KJV).

Any prolonged affliction on any child of God, especially a recurring one should be fought based on the covenant word of God. It is good to know in fact that there were no cancer, heart or kidney failures or other terminal diseases in the Garden of Eden when God created man. It was sin that gave birth to affliction.

By redemption through the blood of Jesus, you are the seed of the righteous, the heirs of God and co-heirs with Christ according to promise. He took your infirmities to the cross and made an open show of them as we read in Colossians 2:15 KJV:

"And having spoiled principalities and powers, he made a shew of them openly, triumphing over them in it."

It is the satanic condemnation, because of either our ignorance or carelessly dwelling in a sinful act, which opens the door to afflictions. Yet the Bible assures us that:

"There is therefore now no condemnation to them which are in Christ Jesus, who walk not after the flesh, but after the Spirit." (Rom. 8:1 KJV)

There should be no condemnation (no adjudging guilty of wrong) for those who are in Christ Jesus, who live and walk not after the dictates of the flesh, but after the Spirit. There should be no physical condemnation on the account of infirmities, e.g., cancer. Cancer can affect every organ in the human body and many cancer victims are made to go through invasive surgeries or are amputated if it affects the exterior parts of the body.

Beloved, Jesus was condemned to death so that no part of your body should be condemned on the account of infirmities. This is because your body is the temple of God, and He dwells inside of you. If you are facing this trouble, being diagnosed of any form of ailments, begin to resist, and declare your healing now using the word of God because according to Psalm 107:20 KJV: *"He sent his word, and healed them..."*.

1. **Present your strong reasons through the declaration of God's word.**

The following are Biblical references that you can stand on in prayer. You must spend time meditating or ruminating on them as you spend time with the Lord in prayer. Our Father is a great God, and He gives good gift. We are clearly told in James 1:17 that KJV:

"Every good gift and every perfect gift is from above, and cometh down from the Father of lights, with whom is no variableness, neither shadow of turning."

For the above reason it is important to trust the Lord for the gift of healing as we are assured in the scriptures quoted below:

"For I will restore health unto you And heal you of your wounds, says the LORD...." (Jer. 30:17 NKJV)

"Behold, I will bring it health and cure, and I will cure them, and will reveal unto them the abundance of peace and truth." (Jer. 33:6 KJV)

"And the LORD will take away from you all sickness, and will afflict you with none of the terrible diseases of Egypt which you have known, but will lay them on all those who hate you." (Deut. 7:15 NKJV).

These and many other scriptures will help you to fight the enemies, secure the quickest answer to your prayer, and grant you victory. But the problem now is that many believers do not know how to make use of the valuable and most dependable resources that are embedded in the word of God. Some see the word of God as a story book because this and that happened in that time, and it cannot happen now. I have heard a Christian saying healings only happened in the time of Christ and the Apostles. Many fail to understand that Jesus paid the price for our healing on the cross. The Bible declares that:

"who Himself bore our sins in His own body on the tree, that we, having died to sins, might live for righteousness-- by whose stripes you were healed." (1 Pet. 2:24 NKJV)

The phrase *"..you were healed"* is a past tense, which implied the fact that Jesus paid it all for you on the cross of Calvary. He took your sins the cause of sickness, and gave you the power to do exploits as you believe:

"Verily, verily I say unto you; He that believeth on me, the works

that I do shall he do also; and greater works than these shall he do, because I go unto my Father." (Jn. 14:12 KJV) .

Until you see the word of God as a living force, and the power that be, the enemy will still defeat you. The scripture in Hebrews 4:12 KJV the Bible says, "***the word of God is quick***" which in the Greek language means it is "alive, living, and lively" and "***powerful***" means "full of energy, energized, active, and effective." It further means that the word that is released is so active, energized, and full of life to act faster to accomplish the purpose you sent it to achieve. The passage also added some powerful thoughts which is that it can conduct the "***...dividing asunder of soul and spirit, and of the joints and marrow,...***"

The suggestion here is that if you have a surgery appointment in the hospital, take time to meditate on God's word and allow it to be established and rooted in your heart. You can in the process declare in your heart saying with strong reasons:

"**Father, I believe your word is true I'm not afraid of this surgery, I believe you, O Lord.**"

Your declaration is founded on the fact that God knows who you are and how you were created as we read in Psalm 139:15-16 KJV and you will be justified to do so:

"***My substance was not hid from thee, when I was made in secret...Thine eyes did see my substance, yet being unperfect; and in thy book all my members were written, Which in continuance were fashioned, when as yet there was none of them.***"

You should declare the result of the surgery in faith after you key into the word of God, and you will be amazed about the power in the word of God when it helps you to reach your desired expectation. The reason you do not experience it before is because of what Apostle James tells us: "***...ye have not, because ye ask not.***" (Jas. 4:2 KJV)

2. His promises still stand.

The promises of God are rich for those who dare to ask.

"***Do not be deceived, God is not mocked; for whatever a man sows, that he will also reap.***" (Gal. 6:7 KJV).

Therefore, sow the word of God in prayer today and reap the desired victories in Jesus' name. He has promised that "*I will not leave you comfortless: I will come to you.*" (Jn. 14:18 KJV)

"*Then shalt thou call, and the LORD shall answer; thou shalt cry, and he shall say, Here I am….*" (Is. 58:9 KJV)

Understand that Jesus is the only great physician and the Omniscient (All Knowing) who specializes in all fields. He has hundred percent solution to every problem with guarantee. I never heard that Jesus lost any patient, neither did He ever refer a patient to another specialist no matter how critical the patient's condition may be. He always has answer to every problem or situation. You have not experienced this because "*ye ask not*" (Jas 4:2 KJV).

3. Lack of faith

The Bible tells us to resist the devil, and what does this mean? Many Christians erroneously think that their will power or determination will suffice the power of the devil. Others believe that a loud shout at the devil would scare him away, while others think formulas they thought in their heads and invoked would solve the problem. Even though to gain the ability to resist the power of darkness will require faith, the result will surely be great.

Resisting the devil is to stand firm in faith. A solid walk, in faith is a strong defense against the devil. Resisting the devil includes drawing nigh to God and living a life of humility:

"….."*God resists the proud, But gives grace to the humble.*" (Jas. 4:6 NKJV)

In Ephesians 6:10-11 Paul says:

"*Finally, my brethren, be strong in the Lord, and in the power of his might. Put on the whole amour of God, that ye may be able to stand against the wiles of the devil.*"

This is because the weapons of our warfare are not carnal but mighty through God to the pulling down of strongholds (2 Cor 10:3-5 NKJV). Although the apostles were living in the flesh, yet they did not wage spiritual warfare in the flesh. So, in using the word to resist the devil, you must establish confidence in God and be fully persuaded that Christ is able to get you the needed solution.

"And this is the confidence that we have in him, that, if we ask any thing according to his will, he heareth us: and if we know that he hear us, whatsoever we ask, we know that we have the petitions that we desired of him." (1Jn. 5:14-15 KJV)

As mentioned earlier, the word of God is the most powerful, sharper, and quickest weapon that believers should use to bring down the power of darkness (Heb 4:12 KJV). The word of God when deployed is instantaneous and the result is right before us. For example, a noble person said to Jesus come down my child is dying. *"Jesus said unto him, Go thy way; thy son liveth.."* (Jn 4:50 KJV).

The man went home believing and yet unknown to him the word had already traveled ahead of him as was confirmed in John 4:51.

"As he was now going down, his servants met him, and told him, saying, Thy son liveth."

The nobility in his curiosity *"Then enquired he of them the hour when he began to amend. And they said unto him, Yesterday at the seventh hour the fever left him."* (vs. 52 KJV).

The speed at which this word traveled is incomprehensible. A scientific study shows that the speed at which light and all electromagnetic radiation travel show about 300,000 kilometers per second or 186,000 miles per second. We cannot compare this with the living force, which is the word of God because *"...the words that I speak unto you, they are spirit, and they are life."* (Jn. 6:63 KJV).

The word is so powerful that it can shake the whole earth and turn the world upside down. In Hebrews 12:26 we read:

"whose voice then shook the earth: but now he hath promised, saying, Yet once more I shake not the earth only, but also heaven." (Heb. 12:26 KJV)

You can see the forces embedded in the word of God and how it caused heaven to quake. God is removing every obstacle that causes frustrations, or whatever is molesting you, the unchangeable situations, shackles of poverty, sickness and diseases, and every negative force that troubles you. The promise of God *"...yet once more.."* indicates the final removal and transformation of all that can be shaken – that is, of that which has been created – in order that what cannot be shaken may remain and continue.

Let us consider the following example of things that are shaken. For example, God formed man of the dust of the ground, and breathed into his nostrils the breath or spirit of life. God never created man with the expectation that his body, soul, and spirit will be tormented by sickness. He created man with the supernatural ability to use all the resources in the service of God and for him to operate in dominion. Every living creature that moves upon the earth is expected to submit to man according to Genesis 1:28 KJV:

"And God blessed them, and God said unto them, Be fruitful, and multiply, and replenish the earth, and subdue it: and have dominion over the fish of the sea, and over the fowl of the air, and over every living thing that moveth upon the earth."

Many destinies have gone unfulfilled, disfigured, and become destitute because they failed to operate in dominion. Because man refused to remove the things that are shaken; therefore, the foundations of their marriages are shaken, and divorce kicks in. The ignorance of some of God's own children inspired the enemy to deploy satanic devices to steal, kill and destroy them. They give access to the devil to distort the divine plan of God, but the good news is that the final removal and transformation of all that can be shaken have already been decreed.

For instance, God took Ezekiel in a vision into the valley of dry bones, and Ezekiel reported that:

"The hand of the LORD was upon me, and carried me out in the spirit of the LORD, and set me down in the midst of the valley which was full of bones, and caused me to pass by them round about: and, behold, there were very many in the open valley; and, lo, they were very dry. And he said unto me, Son of man can these bones lives? And I answered, O Lord GOD, thou knowest. Again he said unto me, Prophesy upon these bones, and say unto them, O ye dry bones, hear the word of the LORD." (Ezek. 37:1-4 KJV)

When Jesus went into the mountain to pray the devil went and showed Jesus all the kingdoms of the world and Jesus said to him: "… *Get thee behind me, Satan: for it is written, Thou shalt worship the LORD thy God, and him only shalt thou serve.*" (Lk. 4:8 KJV).

When you begin to use the appropriate word of God to tackle any situation or mountain of prey over your life it will be uprooted. The word is a potent weapon of war that will always get you the desired result when properly deployed at the right time. We are told in 1 Chronicles 12:32 KJV:

"*..Issachar: 200 leaders, together with the men under their command (these leaders knew what Israel should do and the best time to do it);*" (GNV)

This scripture makes us to understand that "*these leaders knew what Israel should do and the best time to do it.*" These leaders not only know what to do, they also know the best time to do it. Knowing the best time to strike the enemy is very crucial in warfare, whether physical or spiritual!

Furthermore, not only is the word of God a potent weapon, but it is also a heavenly scanner that can quickly scan your system and expose every hidden sickness or lie of the devil. As best rendered in Hebrews 4:12 KJV it "*is a discerner of the thoughts and intents of the heart.*" It is a revealer of secrets. Therefore, be prepared to spend time in the word, studying and meditating on it as much as you can in prayer. It is whatever you have inside of you that you can deploy as a weapon of offense in the day of battle. Once more, be warned! "*Be not deceived; God is not mocked: for whatsoever a man soweth, that shall he also reap*" (Gal. 6:7 KJV)

When you heed this advice, you would be like Peter who at the Beautiful Gate without any regret boldly declared, "*…Silver and gold have I none; but such as I have give I thee: In the name of Jesus Christ of Nazareth rise up and walk.*" (Act 3:6 KJV).

So do all you can to acquire grace and the firepower to unseat the operations of the devil in your lives. Spend time in the word and prayer and expect glorious results in Jesus' name, Amen.

CHAPTER FOUR

PRAYING IN FAITH

"And he said to unto her, Daughter, be of good comfort: thy faith hath made thee whole; go in peace." (Lk. 8:48 KJV).

1. The potency of Faith

Faith is a very potent force in all meaningful spiritual activity believers engage in. The reason is without faith no one can please God (Heb 11:6 KJV). For practical purpose, the Lord Jesus taught His disciples the importance of faith as a foundational guide in fulfilling kingdom assignments. We cannot have access to kingdom experience, and neither can we enjoy enormous blessings that come through faith in His name until we encounter Him and testify of His goodness.

The Lord never misses the opportunity to refer to the faith of the person who encounters Him for divine help. The issue of faith to Him is central to the needed solution. For example, He said to the centurion ***"...Go thy way; and as thou hast believed, so be it done unto thee..."*** (Matt. 8:13 KJV). Then in the case of the two blind men who needed His help in Matthew 9:27-28 KJV after asking them the salient question ***"..Believe ye that I am able to do this?"*** and they answered in the affirmative ***"Yea, Lord"*** (Matt. 9:28 KJV). He thereafter responded by touching their eyes and He said: ***"...According to your faith be it unto you."*** (Matt. 9:29 KJV). And, to the woman with the issue of blood,

"...he said to her, Daughter, be of good comfort: thy faith hath made thee whole; go in peace." (Lk. 8:48 KJV).

The three scriptures in reference above reveal the potency of the faith of the recipients of divine visitations from above. Each of them never doubted the Master's word but responded in agreement by going ahead to comply with His instructions in real-time. The Centurion, requested for Him to just speak and he believed his servant would be made whole. We read in the same verse just as he had believed that *"And his servant was healed in the selfsame hour."* (Matt 8:13 KJV). That is potent faith at work.

The emphasis of the Master is always to encourage them not to doubt, because doubt negates the answer to prayers. Apostle James pointedly addressed this issue of doubt headlong in James 1:5-8 KJV:

"If any of you lack wisdom, let him ask of God, that giveth to all men liberally, and upbraideth not; and it shall be given him. But let him ask in faith, nothing wavering. For he that wavereth is like a wave of the sea driven with the wind and tossed. For let not that man think that he shall receive any thing of the Lord. A double minded man is unstable in all his ways."

Faith is a creative power, while doubt is the graveyard of miracles unfulfilled. To always get quick answer to your prayers you must work on your faith by watching what you hear and see.

"So then faith cometh by hearing, and hearing by the word of God." (Rom. 10:17 KJV).

You can also increase the potency of your faith through meditation on the word of God and you shall have good success (Josh. 1:8 KJV)

Faith is a potent force, and one cannot overemphasize it enough as the Lord Jesus did in His days. Again, in Matthews 21:21 KJV we see another reference to this same fact:

"Jesus answered and said unto them, Verily I say unto you, If ye have faith, and doubt not, ye shall not only do this which is done to the fig tree, but also if ye shall say unto this mountain, Be thou removed and be thou cast into the sea; it shall be done." (Matt. 21:21 KJV).

The Lord again on this subject in Mark 9:23 KJV says *"if thou canst believe, all things are possible to him that believeth.*" Therefore, the prayer of faith is necessary because it is having absolute confidence in His name. It is important to also say that everyone who confesses Jesus Christ as Lord and Savior, should know that no amount of good works you have done can substitute or compensate for lack of faith in Him.

The word faith has a twofold sense in the Bible:

i) "Trust," "reliance" and
ii) "Fidelity,"

In Roman 3:3 KJV, the bible says
"For what if some did not believe? Shall their unbelief make the faith of God without effect?"

To have faith in God, is not a religious idea but doctrinal teaching based on inspirational power that produces a tremendous result. It is not a mental assertion, nor an agreement based on your mindset. Whether you believe or not that does not negate the purpose of God (Rom. 3:3 KJV).

Take note of this, we are not talking about only faith that saves but faith that keeps you in life and living. The evidence of your faith is seen in the outcome of what you are believing God for. There must be evidence in the fruit of your faith - the works or outcome. "*...my brethren, though a man say he hath faith, and have not works? Can faith save him?*" (Jas. 2:14 KJV)

Your faith without evidence of works cannot save you because any faith that does not produce an evidential result is dead. "*But wilt thou know, O vain man, that faith without works is dead?*" (Jas. 2:20 KJV)

If your faith is limited to salvation or saving faith, please know that even demons have that kind of faith:
"*Thou believest that there is one God; thou doest well: the devils also believe, and tremble.*" (Jas. 2:19 KJV).

Therefore, step up your faith, pray, fast, study and meditate on God's word.

Faith is not a strategy to manipulate God, and not a will power by which we make God do what we want him to do. It is also not a magic wand through which we can gain recognition in the church. To exercise domineering power in the church is not faith but rebellion and resistance to God's word. Apostle John identified this kind of bad attitude in the life of Diotrephes, when he wrote in 3 John 1:9 KJV:

"I wrote unto church; but Diotrephes, who loved to have preeminence among them, receiveth us not."

John's letter to the church was mis-interpreted by Diotrephes who had an exaggerated view of his importance and hence resisted him. Many Christians assume that giving donation for the support of spreading the gospel will gain them recognition and that it could compensate for their faith. This is not true! The Bible in Hebrews 11:1 KJV defines faith as the "*...substance of things hoped for, the evidence of things not seen.*"

To have faith in God is to be fully convinced of the truthfulness, reliability, and validity of what He says He is. This is to establish confidence with your Maker that can get you out of every crooked path. Faith denotes the ground of confidence, assurance, guarantee or proof. It is the quality of your faith that leads you to stand and endure, or undertake something in firmness, boldness, and confidence in Christ (2 Cor. 9:1-5 KJV).

In the teachings of Paul, he expressively made us to understand that faith is trusting in the person of Jesus, the truth of His teachings, and the redemptive work He accomplished at Calvary. This is not to be confused with our mere intellectual acceptance. This is because faith in Christ includes a radical and total commitment to Christ as the Lord of one's life. A faith person is a risk-taker, who is willing to damn the consequence because he believes in the saving power of God, especially where God's word or his faith in Him is challenged. We see an exceptionally good example of this in Daniel 6:10 KJV:

"Now when Daniel knew that the writing was signed, he went into his house; and his windows being open in his chamber toward Jerusalem, he kneeled upon his knees three times a day, and prayed, and gave thanks before his God, as he did aforetime."

Daniel, committed himself to the cause, refused to bow to pressure and prayed in faith to God. Faith is required to resist the enemy and win the battles of life.

"*And Jesus said unto them, Because of your unbelief: for verily I say unto you, if ye have faith as a grain of mustard seed, ye shall say unto this mountain, Remove hence to yonder place; and it shall remove; and nothing shall be impossible unto you.*" (Matt. 17:20 KJV).

The Lord in the passage above and Mark 11:23 KJV reveal that faith is the key to our relationship with Christ, and the factor that makes Christianity different. Faith beautifies and dignifies the saints. It is a force that supernaturally empowered the three Hebrew boys to boldly declare to the King: "*...we are not careful to answer thee in this matter. If it be so, our God whom we serve is able to deliver us from the burning fiery furnace, and he will deliver us out of thine hand, O king*" (Dan. 3:16-17 KJV).

The three Hebrew boys were saying in faith to the King if you have anything more grievous than casting us to burning fiery furnace do it now because we are not going to bow to your idol. These men were not just saying their minds because they were eloquent, no, they were speaking the word of God in faith because they knew their God and the scripture confirm that:

"*...the people who [are spiritually mature and] know their God will display strength and take action [to resist]*" (Dan. 11:32 AMP).

These three courageous men led a heroic revolt against the King's decree. Their exploits against inexplicable odds, were nothing short of the phenomenon. The fact was that they knew their God laid hold of His sovereign power and might, acted and looked unto Him to deliver them. Their story reveals faith in God, and how much they believe in His mighty power. They did extraordinary things because they knew God. Jude 1:3 KJV truly and boldly confirms that: a spirit of faith "*...was once delivered to the saints.,*" that is all those who believe."

2. What produces faith?

"And he spake many things unto them in parables, saying, Behold, a sower went forth to sow; and when he sowed, some seeds fell by the way side, and the fowls came and devoured them up: some fell upon stony places, where they had not much earth: and forthwith they sprung up, because they had no deepness of earth: and when the sun was up, they were scorched; and because they ho root, they withered away. And some fell among thorns; and the thorns sprung up, and choked them: but other fell into good ground, and brought forth fruit, some an hundredfold, some sixtyfold, some thirtyfold." (Matt. 13:3-8 KJV)

In the parable of the Sower, the Lord Jesus describes four different types of soil. The soil which is symbolic of the heart affects the output of the seed. The good soil or heart produces good fruits, while the bad correspondingly produces bad fruits. In the parable, the seed which is the word of God was scattered into various kinds of soil and they all produced diverse kinds of results. We are going to examine below the different conditions of soils:

a) The Wayside

The wayside or the roadside kind of soil is the hard soil where people constantly walk. It is so hard that nothing can penetrate or sink into it and therefore the seed vulnerably stays on the surface at the risk of pedestrians trampling on it or the birds of the air devouring it. This soil is beaten by every passing foot; therefore, nothing will ever grow on it. The same is true of the wayside Christian who has nothing to offer because it retains nothing in his heart. Inexplicably, his heart is bombarded by massive or array of conflicting but compelling worldly arguments based on human logic (flesh) rather than the content of the spirit (i.e., the word that makes free - John 8:31-32 KJV).

Well, known to all is the fact that, the word comes and hits a hard heart bouncing back without penetrating it for change. Hard heart resists the word by relegating it to the level of the world by declaring the power of the flesh to be much more logical than that of the spirit. Hard heart believes that making wealth only comes through arduous work laced with smart crookedness. Yet the Bible tells us that:

"The blessing of the LORD, it maketh rich, And he addeth no sorrow with it." (Prov. 10:22 KJV).

In fact, God specifically and unequivocally said to Israel:

"But thou shalt remember the Lord thy God: for it is he that giveth thee power to get wealth,....." (Deut. 8:18 KJV).

Becoming wealthy is part of the covenant promise God made to the fathers so no man operating outside of this covenant can enjoy true prosperity. True prosperity is well defined in 3 John 1:2 KJV and they are: *"Beloved, I wish above all things that thou mayest prosper and be in health, even as thy soul prospereth."* The breakdown of this verse is itemized below:

i)   Financial prosperity
ii) Prosperity of our health
iii) Prosperity of long life or life fully lived.

If any of these three is missing, you are neither wealthy nor prosperous you are simply rich, but it would not last. Therefore, let God be the foundation of your prosperity by working on the soil of your heart!

d)   The shallow soil or Rocky ground

They *"..immediately received it* (the word) *with gladness."* (Mk 4:16 KJV)

This heart is the hot-headed or frivolous one that quickly responds to the word without the core energy to follow through. It is a rolling stone that gathers no moss. Those with these hearts are loud and very showy but they lack depth!

Even though the seed in this type of soil can sink into the heart of the soil and sprout, unfortunately, the soil is shallow with rock underneath therefore it has no deep root. It lasts only for a short time.

The example of spiritual stamina to fight is seen in the case of Abraham resisting the enemy that wanted to steal the tokens of his covenant with the Lord, but he stood his ground by fighting them with all he had (Gen. 15:11-12 KJV)!

"And when the birds of prey swooped down upon the carcasses, Abram drove them away. When the sun was setting, a deep sleep overcame Abram, and a horror (a terror, a shuddering fear) of great darkness assailed and oppressed him." (Gen. 15:11-12 AMPC)

But the one who is like a seed on the rocky ground could not endure a challenge like this. When trouble or persecution arises on the account of the word, this one quickly collapses under pressure because he or she has no deep root.

e) Seed sown among thorns

"He also that received seed among the thorns is he that hearth the word; and the care of this world, and the deceitfulness of riches, choke the word, and he becometh unfruitful." (Matt. 13:22 KJV)

The person who represents this kind of seed faces self-inflicted wounds because of the love of the world. He is surrounded by temptations, and yet he does not watch and pray. He takes these tempting situations for granted and yet he has no core. He loves hearing the word, but he wants to serve both God and Mammon at the same time.

For example, the thorny seed went through the initial stage of hardship; and the care of this world, the worries of life, the deceitfulness of riches and the lust of life distracted him. The gospel of Luke 8:14 KJV describes the challenge he faced as *"the pleasures of this life,"*. This one endured these for a while but because he was not solidly grounded in the word, he could not pass the test. For this reason, his faith was choked by the thorny issues of life. The Bible encourages a believer in 2 Timothy 2:3 KJV to *"... endure harshness, as a good soldier of Jesus Christ."*

Who is a good soldier of Christ? One who knows we are called to fight. The Lord says: *"...I will build my church and the gates of hell shall not prevail against it."* (Matt. 16:18 KJV).

This is a call to war. And to engage in warfare you must be spiritually prepared and ready in word study/meditation, prayer with fasting and intense worship and fellowship retreats!

3. What causes faith to grow?

Having dealt with the various soil conditions, the question we need to ask next is what causes faith to grow? The seed that is sown on a good soil (i.e., good heart) hears the word of God, receives it into his heart, and produces a good crop, some a hundredfold, some sixtyfold, and some thirtyfold (Matt 13:8 KJV). When the word is received with adequate attention in faith, meditated on in the heart and with prayer it bears the fruits of increase. The more you are actively engaged on the word of God you will grow in faith. In John 15:7 KJV we read that: *"If ye abide in me, and my words abide in you, ye shall ask what ye will, and it shall be done unto you."*

When we read the word of God and meditate on it, it produces the powerful force call faith. The Bible makes us to understand that he who meditates on God's word: *"…shall be like a tree planted by the rivers of water, that bringeth forth his fruit in his season; his leaf also shall not wither; and whatsoever he doeth shall prosper."* (Ps. 1:3 KJV).

In fact, Joshua opines that when you meditate day and night, and: *"..observe to do according to all that is written therein: for thou shalt make thy way prosperous, and then thou shalt have good success."* (Josh. 1:8 KJV)

The word of God sown in the heart of a believer with proper care grows as seeds in stages, as instructions are being adhered to as Joshua counseled. As true believers spend time in prayer meditation, worship and praise we see the evidence in growth and for this reason:

"We are bound to thank God always for you, brethren, as it is meet, because that your faith groweth exceedingly…" (2 Thess. 1:3 KJV).

Something must cause faith to grow, and one of these is dedication.

Without total dedication faith cannot grow. The word is nonnegotiable, therefore:

"Study to shew yourself approved unto God, a workman that needeth not to be ashamed, rightly dividing the word of truth." (2 Tim. 2:15 KJV).

CHAPTER FIVE

PRAYING IN JESUS NAME

"And whatsoever ye shall ask in my name, that will I do, that the Father may be glorified in the Son." (Jn. 14:13 KJV)

A. Background

The name Jesus is the source of power and authority for believers. God gave Him a name that is above every name for the reason of the fact that He was humble as a man and became obedient unto death, even the death on the cross (Phil 2:8), He did not just get the name on a platter of gold, He paid the ultimate price and power was attributed to that name. The value of the power and strength He holds is predicated on His name, and He clearly confirms it to His willing hearers that:

"....*All power is given to me in heaven and in earth*" (Matt. 28:18 KJV).

No one could contest that fact because "*God hath spoken once; Twice have I heard this; That power belongeth unto God.*" (Ps. 62:11 KJV). Not just the fact that He only has the ultimate power, beyond that: "*Also unto thee, O Lord, belongeth mercy: for thou renderest to every man according to his work.*" (v12)

For the name of Jesus to work for you, it must be activated on the grounds of righteousness and living in holiness! While righteousness is imputed; holiness is worked at. No wonder Philippians 2:12 KJV encourages us to "*...work out your own salvation with fear and trembling.*"

Praying in the name of Jesus places a seal that authenticates your requests for speedy answer. He assures us in John 14:13 KJV when we ask in His name, He will answer so that the Father may be glorified in the Son. The name of Jesus is the key that authenticates your request in prayer. The formula for result-oriented kingdom prayer is to operate in the power and authority of Jesus. The Lord Jesus Christ is the only authorizing power that brings us assurance of answer to our prayers. He has the keys of life and death in His hands, and He confirms it by saying,

"*I am he that liveth, and was dead; and behold, I am alive forevermore, Amen; and have the keys of hell and death.*" (Rev 1:18 KJV).

The one exercising His authority can speak boldly to the things in the universe, the heavenly and the earthly realms, in His name. We see a good example in the case of Peter in Acts 3:6 KJV saying: "*...Silver and gold have I none; but such as I have give I thee: In the name of Jesus Christ of Nazareth rise up and walk.*"

The one he prayed for, got instantly healed at the call of that name!

In the context of the power and authority He wields, Jesus ascended into heaven; and is seated on the right hand of God the Almighty Father. From there He declared the power and authority He has. Beyond possessing these powers, He delegated them to His children, the body of Christ in Mark 16:15 KJV telling them, "*Go ye into all the world and preach the gospel to every creature.*" And furthermore, He promised,

"*And these signs shall follow them that believe; In my name shall they cast out devils; they shall speak with new tongues;*" (Mk. 16:17 KJV).

1. The mystery of the name of Jesus

"*Wherefore God hath highly exalted him and given a name which is above every name: that at the name of Jesus every knee shall bow, of things in heaven, and things in earth, and things under the earth.*" (Phil. 2:9-10 KJV).

The scriptures repeatedly reveal that all things are working in His name, and because at the call of His name "*..every knee should bow...*" The breakdown of these is that:

i) Devils are powerless against it (Luke 10:17 KJV),

ii) Demons are cast out in His name (Mark 16:17 KJV), iii) Healing is done in his name (Acts 3:16) and

iii) Salvation comes in His name (Acts 4:12; Rom 10:13 KJV).

iv) We are to be baptized in His name (Acts 2:38 KJV).

v) Jesus commanded us to pray in His name and the Apostles having understood the mystery of His name made incredible impacts through it.

According to Acts 3:6-8 NKJV, after the ascension of Christ, supernatural miracles occurred immediately through Apostle Peter. Also, in Acts 9:34 (NKJV) we read how he met a man called Aeneas and he prayed over him, and he was instantly healed:

"*And Peter said to him, "Aeneas, Jesus the Christ heals you. Arise and make your bed." Then he arose immediately.*"

Without any doubt "*The name of the Lord is a strong tower: the righteous runneth into it, and is safe.*" (Prov. 18:10 KJV). Surely, Christ is the embodiment of His name.

2. Value and worth of Jesus' name

Have you read any passage in the gospels where Jesus Himself used His name? He told His disciples to pray to the Father in His Name. When He, Jesus, prayed to the Father, whose name did He use? Did He go to the Father and pray in His name? Certainly not! Jesus does not pray in His name He is the embodiment of that name. When God highly exalted the name of Jesus, Jesus as a Person was exalted. However, God gave Him an exalted name that is above every other name, so that other people can use it to partake of His life (Phil. 2:9-11 KJV).

In other words, Jesus' name is not for His own use. His Name is for His followers to use. Therefore, through His name, any man who believes in Him can fully enjoy all the privileges of the person of Jesus Himself. In other words, the name is a mystery that connects people to partake of the life of Christ!

When you go to the Father and pray in the name of Jesus, the Father hears but it is Jesus making the request through you! The name of Jesus has brought you into the privileges of Christ. That is why your prayers in faith and in line with the will of God cannot be denied. You do not have to struggle or beg. You have the name of Jesus that grants you access to grace (Rom. 5:1-2 KJV)!

When you speak to demons, the reason they come out is because it is not your voice they hear. As you speak in the name of Jesus, your voice becomes the very voice of Christ extended and that is what demons hear and they immediately recognize the power and authority of the Lord Jesus and therefore flee.

Jesus says that name has been given to you for your use. Imagine your father giving you his debit or credit card to use, and you go to a store to purchase anything you want with it, the financial record will not show that you bought something from that store. The financial record will show that your father did because you are simply enjoying the privileges of your father! In the same manner, Jesus has given you His bank card! He has entrusted His name to you. Therefore, enjoy the privileges of Jesus the Son of the living God!

3. Meditate on the word

Meditation on God's word helps you to fully appropriate the benefits of what the name of Jesus has in store for you. When you meditate you become like a tree planted by the rivers of water that bringeth forth his fruit in his season (Ps 1:3 KJV). Through meditation you will prosper and have good success (Josh. 1:8 KJV).

Now who benefits from the exaltation of Jesus?

Let us review Ephesians 1:22 KJV

"and hath put all things under his feet, and gave him to be the head over all things to the church,"

The truth is the church, and we are that church. While all things are under the feet of Jesus, when we exercise His authority, all things are also under our feet too.

4. Apply the Word

Do you trust the name of Jesus? Do you believe that prayer by default should be struggle-free? There is no mystery in making God answer your prayers. He has given you, His name. Therefore, learn to live completely in His name, that is, living fully in Christ. Learn to live His life, and not yours. Do all you can to *".... live, and move, and have your being;..."* in Him (Acts 17:28 KJV).

As you spend your time in His word, you will connect with the key that opens all doors. He categorically said to Peter:

"And I will give unto thee the keys of the kingdom of heaven: and whatsoever thou shall bind on earth shall be bound in heaven: and whatsoever thou shall loose on earth shall be loosed in heaven." (Matt. 16:19 KJV).

Jesus gave the keys of the kingdom of heaven to Peter. That means, Peter received the authority to unlock the revelation of God's word. God uses His creation as agent to accomplish His purpose on earth. He does nothing without human agent and so He delegates His authority to humankind to function in every area of life. For instance, the Lord after He created the beast of the field and the fowl of the air brought them unto Adam: *"...to see what he would call them: and whatever Adam called every living creature that was the name thereof."* (Gen. 2:19 KJV).

That meant that he had the authority to name everything on earth without any form of opposition, but Adam gave this privilege away through disobedience. Specifically, he transferred delegated authority to Satan, and thereby making humankind to be under his dominion. However, I give all glory to God who sent His only begotten son Jesus to redeem us and restore us to God through his blood (Rev 5:9-10 KJV). He delivered us from the dominion of Satan through the death and resurrection of the Lord Jesus. So now we are free and should do all we can never to return to bondage. Glory be to God!

CHAPTER SIX

THE ISSUE OF THE HEART

*"**Keep thy heart with all diligence; for out of it are the issues of life.**"* (Prov. 4:23 KJV)

The issue of the heart is so important for the survival of every believer because our heart is the path to our access to God.

*"**For with the heart man believeth unto righteousness;...**"* (Rom. 10:10 KJV)

Without the right heart no one could have access to God. God is nigh unto such are of a broken heart and saves those who have the contrite spirit (Ps. 34:18 KJV). It is important to know that the heart is the center of our being and that is why we are told to guard our hearts *"**with all diligence; for out of it are the issues of life.**"* (Prov. 4:23 KJV)

Our heart is the core of who we are and the source where all decision is taken. When it comes to seeking God for an answer, the topic of purity is a heart issue and God is looking for those with pure heart. *"**Blessed are the pure in heart: for they shall see God**"* (Matt. 5:8 KJV).

Without pure heart or holiness no man can see Him (Heb. 12:14). Hence, it is important to:

*"**Draw nigh to God, and he will draw nigh to you. Cleanse your**

hand, ye sinner; and purity your hearts ye double minded." (Jas. 4:8 KJV).

The word of God links purity of heart to righteous life to show that those who honor God more than anything else will have direction on how they live their lives. Purity flows from a heart that has been transformed and cleansed by the love of God. No matter how hard you try, you cannot disconnect your sexual behaviors from your heart. The gospel of Matthew 5 verse 8 recorded that only the pure in heart can see God. James also echoes those with clean hands and a pure heart can draw near to God. That implies that a pure heart is cleansed from sin through the sacrificial blood of Jesus Christ.

It is those who accept Jesus as their LORD and Savior who have been given new hearts because old things are passed away and all things have become new that can experience pure hearts (2 Cor. 5:17 KJV). The issue of the heart is so important to God that all through the Bible His desire is to give us new hearts or hearts of flesh to replace stony hearts. For example, in Ezekiel 36:26 KJV we read one of such profound promises:

"A new heart also will I give you, and a new spirit will I put within you: and I will take away the stony heart out of your flesh, and I will give you an heart of flesh" (Ezek. 36:26 KJV).

Beloved, you cannot claim to be a believer and possess hard or stony heart. The evidence of your salvation is clearly revealed in how pure your heart is. Therefore, purity of heart is found in those who have truly repented of their sins. It is no wonder that King David, wanting to be right with God, cried out in desperation in Psalm 51:10 KJV:

"Create in me a clean heart, O God; And renew a right spirit within me."

Having this attitude and backing it with sincere heartfelt prayers is the beginning of the journey to the purity of heart. Furthermore, the Psalmist in Chapter 66 verses 18 further declares the power and the value of the contents of the heart in the place of prayer.

"If I regard iniquity in my heart, The LORD will not hear me." (Ps. 66:18 KJV).

This means if I have deliberately indulged or engaged in iniquity;

if I have a wicked end in view; if I have not been willing to forsake all sin; and if I have cherished the ambition for wrongdoing, the Lord will not hear my petition. Therefore, in order that our prayer may be heard, there must be a desire to forsake all forms of sins. Those who continue in their wickedness stand on the verge of being disconnected from God. God is far away from sinners, and when they cry to Him in trouble, He will not hear them. In Psalm 18:41 we read how: ***They cried, but they were none to save them: Even unto the LORD, but he answered them not.***

*"**Then shall they call upon me, but I will not answer; They shall seek me early, but they shall not find me**."* (Prov. 1:28 KJV)

Why will God not hear them? It is because we are told in John 9:31 KJV that:

*"**Now we know that God heareth, not sinners: but if any man be a worshipper of God, and doeth his will, him he heareth**."* (Jn. 9:31 KJV).

All the scriptures quoted pointed to the fact that God will not hear the prayers of sinners. The greatest and most important principle regarding prayer is to draw nigh unto God as we guard our hearts against sins!

The same principle applies to personal purposes of sin, to sinful aspiration, corrupt passion, and evil tendencies. The acts of corruption in an individual's life, as when a man is pursuing a business or a career founded on dishonesty, fraud, oppression and wrong are all explained below:

(a) The public acts of sin, as when a people fast and pray Isaiah 58:1-14, and yet hold their fellowmen in bondage, or enact and maintain unjust and unrighteous laws; or uphold the acts of wicked rulers; or countenance and support by law that which is contrary to the law of God.

(b) To have the feelings of an awakened and trembling sinner when he is seeking salvation. Understand that impurity of the heart cannot give clarity; it makes us blind, deaf, and dumb to the workings of God. Purity leads to clarity, while impurity of heart leads to double-minded idolatry. That means, when our hearts and thoughts are clouded in sins, they lead to ungodliness.

(c) Take a moment and examine your heart: Do you lack spiritual clarity? Are you living in a fog of impurity? Ask God for grace to surrender it all to him (Ezek. 36:25 KJV)

CHAPTER SEVEN

PURITY AND RIGHTEOUSNESS

"Draw nigh to God, and he will draw nigh to you. Cleanse your hands, ye sinners; and purify your hearts, ye double minded." (Jas. 4:8 KJV).

Introduction

The importance of purity is for you to accept the need for the cleansing of your heart from sin which is the work of grace. No one can achieve this through religion, morality or good works or deeds.

He is able, upon repentance, to rid us of all the idols we have enthroned in our hearts. Someone born again cries out for God to do this and He gives them the strength to withstand all temptations and live according to His word.

"And I will put my spirit within you, and cause you to walk in my statutes, and ye shall keep my judgments, and do them." (Ezek. 36:27 KJV).

All that is necessary is for us to come to the Lord and be willing to do what He requires of us is to do in righteousness and truth. How can any person think that he is saved without his willingness for God to cleanse his heart? If he is willing, surely there must be the corresponding obedience that should lead to change of heart!

"Who shall ascend into the hill of the LORD? Or who shall stand in his holy place? He that hath clean hands, and a pure heart; Who hath not lifted up his soul unto vanity, nor sworn deceitfully. He shall receive the blessing from the LORD, And righteousness from the God of his salvation." (Ps 24:3-5 KJV).

We will look at our responsibility in the second part of this study, but it should be abundantly clear that it is impossible to worship God with an impure heart. So, our cry should be:

"Let us draw near with a true heart in full assurance of faith, having our hearts sprinkled from an evil conscience, and our bodies washed with pure water." (Heb. 10:22 KJV).

It is only those who have been thus cleansed who will see God. (Matt. 5:8 KJV). Isaiah realized that impurity of heart would hinder his relationship with God.

"Then said I, Woe is me! for I am undone; because I am a man of unclean lips, and I dwell in the midst of a people of unclean lips: for mine eyes have seen the King, the LORD of hosts." (Is. 6:5 KJV).

His repentance and the cleansing work of God would have been doomed without this, for no man can look upon God and live (Ex. 33:20 KJV). If we do not see our need for the purity of heart, how can we expect to see Him who is holy?

By this we do not mean that we can do anything beyond repentance to receive purity of heart, but to maintain it once it has been given, because believers are expected to show the evidence of it. Our hearts must be full of love as we read below.

"Jesus said to him, *"...Thou shalt love the Lord thy God with all thy heart, and with all thy soul, and with all thy mind. This is the first and great commandment. And the second is like unto it, Thou shalt love thy neighbour as thyself. On these two commandments hang all the law and the prophets."* (Matt. 22:37-40 KJV).

Where there is no such love for God and for people, the heart is void of purity.

"Seeing ye have purified your souls in obeying the truth through

the Spirit unto unfeigned love of the brethren, see that ye love one another with a pure heart fervently." (1 Pet. 1:22 KJV).

Our hearts must be full of faith. This seems like something that all Christians have already, but the sad fact is that the opposite is true. They may know all the details in their heads, but they do not live for the Lord from the heart. The Epistle to the Romans makes us to understand the connection between purity and righteousness by letting us know:

"*that if thou shalt confess with thy mouth the Lord Jesus, and shalt believe in thine heart that God hath raised him from the dead, thou shalt be saved. For with the heart man believeth unto righteousness; and with the mouth confession is made unto salvation.*" (Rom. 10:9-10 KJV).

All mouth and no heart are the spiritual conditions of many today. True faith is found in the heart. Faith that is in the head is simply religion founded on the hall of fame of Mr. Flesh. And as we all know the flesh works death and it is contrary to the spirit – "*...they that are in the flesh cannot please God.*" (Rom. 8:8 KJV)!

Our hearts must be full of honesty. In the parable of the Sower the only ground that received the seed and produced a harvest was the one who had a "*...honest and good heart, having heard the word, keep it, and bring forth fruit with patience*" (Lk. 8:15 KJV).

Paul in Romans 12:17 encourages us to: "*..Provide things honest in the sight of all men.*" Our hearts must be full of humility. Jesus said, "*Verily I say unto you, Except ye be converted, and become as little children, ye shall not enter into the kingdom of heaven. Whosoever therefore shall humble himself as this little child, the same is greatest in the kingdom of heaven.*" (Matt. 18:3-4 KJV).

This virtue is a beautiful trait found in those who have a pure heart.

Conclusion

The scripture above can be expanded to cover other areas of the Christian life, but we at least see that purity of heart is more than just saying we have it. God does the work, but we must live it out in our daily lives and in our interactions with other people.

"*For it is God which worketh in you both to will and to do of his good pleasure.*" (Phil 2:13 KJV).

The righteousness of heart is imputed by God, but it is also evidenced by practical holiness and godly living that must be worked at (Phil. 2:12 KJV). Those who have it will be glorified with Christ.

"*Beloved, now are we the sons of God, and it doth not yet appear what we shall be: but we know that, when he shall appear, we shall be like him; for we shall see him as he is. And every man that hath this hope in him purifieth himself, even as he is pure.*" (1 Jn. 3:2-3 KJV).

CHAPTER EIGHT

THE SPEAKING OF THE BLOOD OF JESUS

"*but ye have come unto mount Zion, and unto the city of the living God, the heavenly Jerusalem, and to an innumerable company of angels, to the general assembly and church of the firstborn, which are written in heaven, and to God the Judge of all, and the spirits of just men made perfect, and to Jesus the mediator of the new covenant, and to the blood of sprinkling, that speaketh better things than that of Abel.*" (Heb. 12:22-24 KJV)

A. The importance of the blood of Jesus

What is important about the Blood of Jesus? The human blood is the life of the person in which it flows. It has identity, and presence and it speaks. We can perfectly relate to this when we remember that in Genesis, when Cain murdered Abel something unusual happened – his blood spoke. However, it would not have been ordinarily known to us until God mentioned it. When He did, He asked Cain a hard question in Genesis 4:9-10 KJV: "*And the LORD said unto Cain, Where is Abel thy brother?*" *And he said, l knows not: Am l my brother's keeper? And he said, What has thou done? the voice of thy brother's blood crieth unto me from the ground."*

From that passage of scriptures, no one would have known about what happened to the blood of Abel until God revealed it. It is God that made us to understand that:

"The voice of thy brother's blood crieth unto me from the ground." (Gen. 4:10 KJV).

Abel's blood cried unto God from the ground and not to man. His blood cried unto the one who could avenge him from the pain of premature death. Briefly, the blood of Abel cried out for vengeance.

In comparison, the blood of Jesus only cries out for mercy. His blood has redeeming qualities better than the blood of rams and goats. It is the blood that guarantees redemptions from death to life; from sickness to health; from bondage to deliverance; and from helplessness to help. It is in Him we have **"..redemption through his blood, the forgiveness of sins, according to the riches of his grace;.."** (Eph. 1:7 KJV).

We further learned from the Bible that as our High Priest He presented His own blood in the holy place as an offering for the redemption of our souls. Our redemption was: **"neither by the blood of goats and calves, but by his blood he entered in once into the holy place, having obtained eternal redemption for us"** (Heb. 9:12 KJV)

For the reason stated above, He became the **"...mediator of the New Testament,"** and the guarantor for the transgressors by acquiring for them **"..the promise of eternal inheritance."** (Heb. 9:15 KJV)

For the sake of clarity, let us clearly consider the Biblical account of the murder of Abel by Cain. As mentioned earlier, until God spoke the Bible does not claim that Abel's blood cried out for vengeance. If God had not mentioned it, no person dead or alive would have known but God willingly revealed it for us to know the gravity of the offence and the consequence! Up until God spoke, no one knows that blood speaks!

Furthermore, we need to know that whatsoever we do in life is a seed and we must without any doubt reap the fruits of it. Let us stop deceiving ourselves, it is whatsoever we sow, that we will reap (Gal 6:9). When Cain offered his sacrifice, he did not do it with the right heart! He did it with contention and competition in mind. God does not look at the gift offered but the heart of the giver. If you bring a bad gift, it reflects your evil heart.

*"**When you offer blind animals for sacrifice, is that not wrong? When you sacrifice lame or diseased animals, is that not wrong? Try offering them to your governor! Would he be pleased with you? Would he accept you?" says the Lord Almighty.*" (Mal. 1:8 NIV).

When you offer polluted sacrifice, you make the table of the Lord become contemptible. (Mal 1:7 KJV)

When Cain brought his offering, his heart was full of jealousy and so he acted in like manner. From that perspective his offering was polluted, and for this reason God rejected it.

Some class of theologians erroneously believe that God rejected his sacrifice because he did not offer something that had blood, which is not correct. You offer to God the fruit of your labor and since Cain was a farmer, he could only have offered his farm produce.

Brethren, watch your heart because God seriously investigates a man's heart (1 Sam. 16:7 KJV). God is nigh only unto those whose hearts are broken (Ps. 34:18 KJV). In fact, we are specifically told in Psalm 51:17 KJV that:

*"**The sacrifices of God are a broken spirit: A broken and a contrite heart, O God, thou wilt not despise.**"*

Cain failed miserably and his sacrifice was despised because of his bad heart. So, watch your heart! Do you harbor evil or wickedness in your heart? If you do, forget it your sacrifice is bound to be despised. May God help us all with our hearts in Jesus' name, amen!

The consequence of Cain's action was far-reaching beyond what an ordinary mind could contemplate. Spiritually speaking, the very day that Cain killed Abel, his brother, he did not just murder one man, but he also truncated the destinies of several generations of people that ought to have come through the lineage of Abel! The Blood of Abel was screaming before God for vengeance because the generations confined within Abel would never be birthed. They all died in his loins with him.

B. Why does the Bible say that the Blood of Jesus speaks better thing than Abel's?

While Abel offered a better sacrifice from the produce of his labor unto God, Jesus offered Himself for our redemption. In the days of Jesus, like Cain, the Pharisees and Sadducees were envious of Jesus, and so with the cooperation of the Romans, the Elders and other Jews sentenced Him to death. When Jesus was brought before Herod, He knew their accusations were rooted in jealousy. The same satanic envy in Cain transferred through the bloodline and manifested in the evil ones to orchestrate the killing of the Prince of life.

When Jesus (the type of Abel) stepped into the land, the same Spirit of Cain came after Him through the evil cooperation of the Pharisees, Sadducees, the Elders, other Jews, and the Roman authority. The difference between the death of Abel and Jesus is that when they killed Jesus, the blood that went before the throne of God did not cry for vengeance but mercy. The biblical account shows that the blood of Jesus speaks for seven major things. We will briefly review them for perspective and clarity.

1. The blood Jesus pleads for Mercy.

The DNA of God speaks of nothing else but His love which is full of mercy. Mercy simply means that when we deserve punishment, He does not punish us; instead, He shows us mercy by forgiving us.

In the Old Testament, anyone who desired mercy must come with two scape goats, "..*and present them before the Lord......And Aaron shall bring the goat upon which the Lord's lot fell, and offer him for a sin offering.*" (Lev. 16:7, 9 KJV)

So, by sacrificing this innocent animal its blood becomes a substitution for his or her sin. So as this animal is substituted for the sinner's sin, mercy kicks in. And the Lord says in Leviticus 17:11 KJV that:

"*For the life of the flesh is in the blood: and I have given it to you upon the altar to make an atonement for your souls: for it is the blood that maketh an atonement for the soul."* (Lev. 17:11 KJV).

In the New Testament, our Lord Jesus Christ ushered in a new covenant through the offering of His own blood.

"For by one offering he hath perfected for ever them that are sanctified." (Heb. 10:14 KJV).

Therefore, the sacrificial offerings of the blood of animals as covenant was expected to have ceased, yet the ignorant ones still offer them!

Beyond this, because every earthly priest does not last for the reason of death, the Lord Jesus in His own case as a Priest, lives forever. He therefore is a *"..surety of a better testament."* And has an *"unchangeable priesthood."* (Heb. 7:22, 24 KJV).

For this reason, *"..he is able to save them to the uttermost that come unto God by him, seeing he ever liveth to make intercession for them."* (Heb. 7:25 KJV)

As mentioned earlier the covenant offering of Jesus is everlasting and His blood speaks better things as we read in Hebrews 12:24 KJV.

"and to Jesus the mediator of the new covenant, and to the blood of sprinkling that speaketh better things than that of Abel."

If the blood of bulls and goats, and the ashes of a heifer sprinkled over the unclean could bring forth the purification of the flesh, what then should you expect of the blood of Christ? Brethren, when we are in covenant with Jesus Christ, we are covered by His blood. His sacrificial blood screams for mercy over our lives. In fact, it was this mercy that made a way for us out of darkness into His marvelous light. Hence, we must understand that everything we acquired in life were acquired through His mercy. There is no more condemnation over our lives because His blood speaks for our forgiveness.

2. The Blood of Jesus speaks Forgiveness of Sins

Forgiveness is an act of pardon you extend or offer to someone who offends you. You are in the process willing to forgo the feelings of resentment or vengeance towards that person or persons, regardless of whether they deserve it or not. It is the letting go of the sin of another by overlooking it that is known as true forgiveness. Forgiveness is an act of willing obedience to God without any let or hindrance. It is not the excusing, forgetting, permitting the repetition of such sinful act against you, or guaranteeing reconciliation with the perpetrator. It is the total cancellation of the person's or persons' sins.

Jesus paid the price for the total cancellation of our sins with His blood on calvary. In Micah 7:18, we see the expression of genuine appreciation of what God has done in showing us mercy:

"Who is a God like unto thee, that pardoneth iniquity, and passeth by the transgression of the remnant of his heritage? He retaineth not his anger forever: because he delighted in mercy." (Mic. 7:18 KJV).

The Bible further makes us to understand that whosoever repents of his sins and knows Him as the Lord and Savior, He will *"forgive and forget"* their sins. He will treat their past offenses as though they never sinned.

"I even I, am He that blotted out thy transgressions for mine own sake and will not remember thy sins." (Is. 43:25 KJV).

The consequence of sins is an indelible and irrevocable mark on the sinner, and it is only the blood of Jesus that can erase and blot it our forever.

3. The blood of Jesus speaks Justification

"Much more then, being now justified by his blood, we shall be saved from wrath through him." (Rom. 5:9 KJV).

By Justification, it means a process through which a person is declared not guilty and acquitted. When a person is absolved from the court of law, he is free from every punishment due to him. We are justified and free from the bondage of Satan, and the blood of Jesus cancels generational sins and curses.

You are no more in bondage to iniquities; and you are acquitted from ignorance that empowers curses to work on you. You are absolved from inherited sickness, free from sudden death; and the blood of Jesus breaks ancestral curses. There is redemption for you in Jesus' name. Amen

It is important to be aware that because of our justification, *"..we have peace with God through our Lord Jesus Christ: By whom also we have access by faith into this grace wherein we stand, and rejoice in the hope of the glory of God."* (Rom. 5:1-2 KJV).

The three important points to note are that:

i) We have peace with God.

ii) We have access into the grace wherein we stand.

iii) We rejoice because we have hope in the glory of His return to take us back to Himself at His coming. Praise the Lord!

4. The blood of Jesus provides protection

"And they shall take of the blood and strike it on the two sides of posts and the upper door post of the houses, wherein they shall eat it. (Ex. 12:7 KJV)

"For I will pass through the land of Egypt this night, and will smite all the firstborn in the land of Egypt, both man and beast; and against all the gods of Egypt I will execute judgment: I am the LORD. And the blood shall be to you for a token upon the houses where ye are: and when I see the blood, I will pass over you, and the plague shall not be upon you to destroy you when I smite the land of Egypt." (Ex. 12:12-13 KJV)

Please make this declaration with me in faith:

"I declare that no destruction shall come near my dwellings. No destructive plagues shall touch me and my household. No weapon formed against me shall prosper, and every tongue that rises against me, be it sickness, or evil plan shall not prosper in Jesus' name."

If the blood of the unblemished animals can spare the children of Israel from plagues, how much more the blood of Jesus Christ which falls like a drop in Gethsemane and flows in a stream from the pierced side as he hung on the cross, and that blood speaks volumes for the faithful. For this reason, you are covered by the protective power of the blood of Jesus. His blood will continue to speak for you in Jesus' name.

5. The blood of Jesus speaks healing for us

"But He was wounded for our transgressions; he was bruised for our iniquities: the chastisement of our peace was upon him, and with his stripes, we are healed." (Is 53:5 KJV).

You are healed because Jesus paid the price for you. Healing is not the work of righteousness; it is the byproduct of the workings of blood of Jesus Christ because by His *"..stripes ye were healed."* (1 Pet 2:24 KJV). Therefore, when you are sick, invoke the power of the blood in Jesus' name. Also declare His sent word to receive your healing (Ps 107:20 KJV) because His wish for you above all things is *"..that thou mayest prosper and be in health, even as your soul prospereth."* (3 Jn. 1:2 KJV)

6. The blood speaks sanctification

"By the which will, we are sanctified through the offering of the body of Jesus Christ once for all." (Heb. 10:10 KJV).

What is sanctification? It is a process through which something is set aside for greater use. This means it is your responsibility to make sure you are set apart. While righteousness is imputed or given, holiness is worked at. You must work out your own salvation with fear and trembling (Phil. 2:12 KJV). No wonder we are encouraged in 2 Timothy 2:21 KJV that: *"If a man, therefore, purge himself from these, he shall be a vessel unto honor, sanctified, and meet for the master's use, and prepared unto every good work."*

If you do not take heed of this advice and are not sanctified, you become a vessel of dishonor not worth being used by the Master. Sanctification made you a royal vessel whereby you gain eternal value.

7. **The blood of Jesus speaks for our redemption**

"In whom we have redemption through his blood, the forgiveness of sins, according to the riches of his grace." (Eph. 1:7 KJV)

To redeem means "to buy back." In reference to Apostle Paul's terminology, this term was specifically about the purchase of a slave's freedom. The concept of this term to Christ's death on the cross is obvious. Because the blood of Jesus Christ redeems us, our initial condition under slavery has changed, and we gained our freedom. Therefore, we are no longer in bondage because:

"Christ hath redeemed us from the curse of the law, being made a curse for us: for it is written, Cursed is every one that hangeth on a tree." (Gal. 3:13 KJV).

For the reasons advanced above, we must do all we can to look unto Jesus the author and finisher of our faith if He tarries. It is well.

CHAPTER NINE

PRAYING IN THE SPIRIT

"praying always with all prayer and supplication in the Spirit, and watching thereunto with all perseverance and supplication for all saints;" (Eph. 6:18 KJV)

A. Praying Always

We have come to the most extremely important subject on the prayer that secures heavenly answers. We understand by the scriptures that the Holy Spirit is the Source and Sustainer of our spiritual life here on earth. Therefore, we need Him to help us in our prayer lives. For every believer, prayer is mandatory, and it should be done always. Therefore, to avoid the chronic unwillingness and ignorance to pray the right way, for the right answer, we need to accept the ministry of the Holy Spirit.

Undoubtedly, the Holy Spirit is the author of prayer, and He is the enhancer and enabler of believers in prayer. The purpose of the Lord is clear about the need for us to receive help in the place of prayer when He promised to send us another comforter in John 14:16. His plan was to send the power to equip the believer to operate at the various levels of prayer. There are the levels of asking, seeking, and knocking which translate to primary, secondary, and tertiary levels of prayers respectively. We see below the seven major areas of help the Holy Spirit provides for believers in their general walk with God and particularly in the place of prayer!

"And I will ask the Father, and He will give you another Comforter (Counselor, Helper, Intercessor, Advocate, Strengthener, and Standby), that He may remain with you forever–" (Jn. 14:16 AMPC)

Let us briefly review the seven interventions of the Holy Spirit for us as we pray

B. The Holy Spirit Interventions in Prayer

1. He helps our infirmities

"Likewise the Spirit also helpeth our infirmities: for we know not what we should pray for as we ought: but the Spirit itself maketh intercession for us with groanings which cannot be uttered." (Rom. 8:26 KJV).

So, in the matter of prayer, the Lord Jesus knows what we should pray for, and knows how we could get answers to prayer. The comforter He sent does exactly that for us by helping our infirmities or weaknesses in prayer because we do not know what we should pray for as we are supposed to. This is the reason believers must engage in the ministry of the Holy Spirit in prayers, to tap into the help He has made available to us.

True prayer must be motivated and inspired by the Holy Spirit. When the Holy Spirit is at the forefront of prayer, such prayer must be according to the will of God (Rom 8:27 KJV). Even in the time of Jesus, we saw the disciples asking for help on how to pray. So, they said to Him, "...*Lord, teach us to pray...*" (Lk. 11:1 KJV).

We are ignorant in prayer, and we do not know what we should ask. Glory be to God, this is where the Holy Spirit the Helper, comes in. Writing on this aspect of the help of the Holy Spirit in Prayer, Andrew Murray said in "The Scent of Prayer, that prayer is God's chosen method for us to communicate with Him (page 9, The Bible Teacher's Guide. Ephesians: Understanding). Further quotation states:

"Just as wonderful and real is the divine work of God on the throne graciously hearing and by His mighty power answering prayer. Just as divine as it is, the work of the Son, interceding and securing and transmitting the answer from above, is the work of the Holy Spirit in us in the prayer that awaits and obtains the answer. The intercession within is as divine as the intercession above."

The explanation here is that there is a connection between our prayer to God through the help of the Holy Spirit, and Christ's intercession for us to God to hear our prayers. There must be oneness in the spirit for heaven to hear our cry. That help is the work of the Holy Spirit to assist those who pray.

2. The Holy Spirit Comforts us through Prayer

One of the major reasons why God made provision for us to pray is because God knows that being a Christian is tough. This tough life is because of the many afflictions that await us, and which could easily make us become discouraged in the race (Ps. 34:19). For this reason, God sent the Holy Spirit to help us overcome trials and challenges in life.

This becomes necessary, especially when you are confronted with a protracted issue in prayer. After you have done all you could in prayer, fasting, sowing seed, and there seems to be no change, it is time to stay in His comforting arms for encouragement! Pure and genuine comfort can only come from God, and this is made available to us through the Holy Spirit.

"And I will pray the Father, and he shall give you another Comforter, that he may abide with you for ever;" (Jn. 14:16 KJV).

Having the Holy Spirit gives us a different mindset that we rarely see in this dying world. Though life may be hard and tough, Christians can still stay confident and hopeful because they have the Holy Spirit indwelling them.

3. The Holy Spirit keeps us connected with God

When we allow Him, the Holy Spirit wants to help us to stay connected with God so that His role as a strengthener could be fulfilled. It is this effort that enables us to develop a more intimate and loving relationship with God the Father and Jesus Christ. It is no doubt we need Him in fulfilling our purpose in prayer as we are encouraged in I John 3:24 KJV:

"Now he who keeps His commandments abides in Him, and He in him. And by this we know that He abides in us, by the Spirit whom He has given us."

4. The Holy Spirit guides us to the Truth

Our weakness and inadequacy in prayer to God is not surprising to our Savior, Jesus Christ. God had never intended that our prayer will linger for quite a while before He answers. So, because of this, He gave us the Holy Spirit that indwells us to instruct, inspire, and illuminate our hearts and minds to pray the will of God. Praying in the Spirit is about articulating the words of God by faith in prayer.

In the book "**Prayer is not much the articulation of words as the posture of the heart**" Page 3 John MacArthur said:

"To pray always is to live in a continual God-consciousness, where everything we see and the experience becomes a kind of prayer, live in deep awareness of and surrender to our heavenly Father."

To obey this exhortation means that, when we are tempted, we hold the temptation before God and ask for His help. When we experience something good and beautiful, we immediately thank the Lord for it. When we see evil around us, we pray that God will make it right and be willing to be used of Him to that end. When we meet someone who does not know Christ, we pray for God to draw that person to Himself and use us to be faithful witnesses. When we encounter trouble, we turn to God as our deliverer. In other words, our life becomes a continual ascending prayer, as we perpetually commune with our heavenly Father through the help of the Holy Spirit who is our guide.

Without the Holy Spirit, we will not be able to see all we perceive and as well know the truth. The Holy Spirit will guide us to discover the truth and see the Bible as how God intended it to be so that we can apply biblical principles in prayer:

"However, when He, the Spirit of truth, has come, he will guide you into all truth; for He will not speak on His own authority, but whatever He hears He will speak; and He will tell you things to come." (Jn. 16:13 NKJV).

5. As we Pray the Holy Spirit convicts us of sin

As we truly engage Him in prayer, He helps us to see obstacle of sins that could hinder answer to our prayers. With His help, we can identify areas of sin we need to settle before we continue to pray. He helps us to differentiate right from wrong, good from evil. He will always remind us of the possible consequences of sin because God does not answer the prayer of sinners (John 9:31). For this reason, the role of the Holy Spirit in convicting us of sin as we pray is very essential to our success in the place of prayer. The Lord's promise is that:

"And when he is come, he will reprove the world of sin, and of righteousness, and of judgment." (Jn. 16:8 KJV).

6. The Holy Spirit allows us to bear righteous Fruit

As you grow intimate with God in prayer and in fellowship with Him, you begin to develop the fruits of the Spirit:

"But the fruit of the Spirit is love, joy, peace, longsuffering, kindness, goodness, faith- fulness, gentleness, self-control. Against such there is no law." (Gal. 5:22-23 NKJV).

The Holy Spirit transforms our lives as we pray and gives us the grace or power that enables us to become more like Jesus. Through the Holy Spirit, we will be able to develop these Christlike traits and reflect Christ's character in our lives. This transformation will never happen without Him and therefore, He transforms us from being carnally minded individuals to spiritually minded Christians.

7. The Holy Spirit imparts spiritual gifts

As we pray in the Holy Spirit and with His help, He imparts spiritual gifts on us.

"Now there are diversities of gifts, but the same Spirit… But the manifestation of the Spirit is given to each one for the profit withal." (1 Cor. 12:4, 7 KJV).

The more time you spend in His presence the greater the impartation. When we go boldly to the throne of grace, we obtain mercy and find grace to help (Heb 4:16 KJV). Through the Holy Spirit, these gifts are given so that we may use it for the will and purpose of God.

C. Conclusion

If we are going to win this spiritual battle, we must continue to always pray in the Spirit. Praying in includes all kinds of prayer and requests. Prayer in general term applies to several types of prayer, but to submit to specific strategy is required to excel in prayer. When such specific command is given by the Holy Spirit, obedience is crucial for you to get the expected outcome. Let us review some examples below:

1. When Israel shouted with a great shout in worship to God while standing outside of Jericho, the city's wall fell as commanded and promised by God (Joshua 6:5 KJV).
2. When Jehoshaphat and the singers worshipped and praised, *"… the Lord set ambushments against.."* their enemies and they were all defeated (2 Chron. 20:22 KJV).
3. When Hannah prayed in her heart with only her lips moving in Shiloh, she was accused of being drunk by Eli, the priest but the Lord heard the cry of her heart. Thereafter, she returned home vindicated with the vision of her Samuel, and it happened as she so desired (1 Sam. 1:12-18 KJV).

Whenever we are tempted to complain and worry, we must remember that we are called to praise and pray in the Spirit.

"What is it then? I will pray with the Spirit, and I will pray with the understanding also: I will sing with the Spirit, and I will sing with the understanding also." (1Cor. 14:15 KJV).

My prayer is that you would get help from Him, and may His Spirit open your eyes to understand this hidden mystery in Jesus' name. Amen.

CHAPTER TEN

THE POWER OF FASTING AS A WEAPON OF SPIRITUAL WARFARE

"I am weary of my crying: my throat is dried:
Mine eyes fail while l wait for my God.
When l wept, and chastened my soul with fasting, That was to my reproach. I made sackcloth also my garment; And I became a proverb to them. They that sit in the gate speak against me; And I was the song of the drunkards. But as for me, my prayer Is unto thee, O LORD, in an acceptable time: O God, in the multitude of thy mercy hear me, in the truth of thy salvation." (Ps. 69:3, 10-13 KJV).

A. Preparing for Warfare

The Psalm of David quoted above reveals to us the intensity and determination required in spiritual warfare. It is not a time to play softball, because what you put in affects the outcome of your prayer exploit. We see how David wept until he was physically exhausted, with a dry throat and blurred vision while he waited for God's intervention on his matter. He cried until he had no more strength, yet he still trusted God to save his life.

When you are devastated by failed expectation, hopelessness, impending or looming death as you wait, you need not give up or despair. You must maintain the fort as you come to God in prayer and fasting. For example, David was scoffed at, mocked, humiliated, insulted, and made an object of ridicule, yet he refused to be discouraged but he held on to God in prayer and fasting.

In spiritual warfare, fasting and prayer must be at the forefront, and you must remember that the enemy you are contending with is vicious. While it is true that all power belongs to God, we must also understand that Satan is a strong man. Just as the Lord Jesus hinted on this subject matter, He said:

"No man can enter into a strong man's house, and spoil his goods, except he will first bind the strong man; and then he will spoil his house." (Mk. 3:27 KJV)

Satan is a strong man, but *"..greater is the one that is in you than he that is in the world."* (1 Jn. 4:4 KJV) And his forces we are fighting against are "principalities and powers." (Eph. 6:12 KJV). These are powerful fallen angels headed by Satan, a vicious fighter. For this reason, we are seriously warned by Apostle Peter in 1Peter 5:8 to: *"Be sober, be vigilant; because your adversary the devil, as a roaring lion, walketh about, seeking whom he may devour."*

As we proceed let us briefly review the beneficial outcomes we get when we wait on God in prayer and fasting. The main point of reference during fasting and prayer is that we draw strength from God as we force the hands of heaven to intervene in our situation. The Holy Spirit takes hold of our weaknesses and replaces them with His strength. And as we wait, several spiritual forces are unleashed to confront us as we fight, but the grace of God is more than sufficient for us and for this reason our victory is guaranteed.

While we briefly review below a few areas where we can use prayer and fasting to address, it is also important to mention that these weapons could be used to confront every challenge of life facing us. Just know that as you grow in their deployments in warfare, you would become well versed in their usage.

1. Fasting for Deliverance

We see a profound example of the deployment of prayer with fasting as formidable weapons of war to guarantee deliverance in Esther 4:16 KJV. There, we read:

"Go, gather together all the Jews that are present in Shushan, and fast ye for me, and neither eat nor drink three days, night or day: I also and my maidens will fast likewise; and so will I go in unto the king, which is not according to the law: and if I perish, I perish."

After the decree to kill the Jews was signed into law, Mordecai and Esther could not just sit and watch. After some deliberations they decided to cry unto to God with fasting for His intervention. This was because, Esther was forced to realize that God had placed her in that position for a purpose. She began with conviction, determination, and request for spiritual support as she engaged herself in the dangerous assignment. Therefore, before she approached the king a fast was proclaimed and the Lord honored her.

Many believe in God's promises but hesitate to act on them in times of trouble. The young Esther and her uncle were willing to suffer affliction with the people of God than to enjoy the pleasures of sin for a season (Heb. 11:25 KJV). They stood in the gap in intercession for their people and God answered their cry. It is good to look unto Jesus as the author and finisher of your faith. So, when you face challenges, seek the face of God in prayer and fasting just as Esther and others did.

2. Fasting for divine intervention

As mentioned earlier, fasting is the source of spiritual power for believers. For example, we read in Mark 9:29 KJV that when the disciples of Christ faced an inconvenient situation and wondered why they could not overcome it, the Lord Jesus told them *"**This kind can come forth by nothing, but by prayer and fasting.**"*

Prayer is the key that activates faith in our lives. Hence, Jesus reminded them that even though we can enjoy breakthroughs in life, yet we must be ready to achieve it through prayer and fasting. If we have been facing unanswered prayer, it may be time to fast and pray. The prayer that is powered by faith and fasting is the only one that can unleash God's divine promises into our lives. This is because without faith it is impossible to please God (Heb 11:6 KJV).

3. Fasting for Miracles

When we lock up ourselves in the throne room to seek the face of God for the issues that may cause shame and reproach in our lives, fasting forces the flesh to come under subjection to the Holy Spirit. When we receive medical reports that place our situations between life and death, and throw us into panic, prayer and fasting are the ways to go. God ordained fasting "...**to loose the bands of wickedness, to undo the heavy burdens...**" (Is. 58: 6 KJV).

Fasting is more than a spiritual exercise; it is meant to make impacts on our situations on earth and transform our circumstances from fear to peace and joy. When we turn to God in fasting, we should not look gloomy as the hypocrites do, for they disfigure their faces to show others that they are fasting (Matt 6:16-18 KJV). While teaching about fasting Jesus, condemned the attitude of looking gloomy because it was done to gain public awareness and approval.

*"**More over when ye fast, be not, as hypocrites, of a sad countenance: for they disfigure their faces, that they may appear unto men to fast. Verily I say unto you, They have their reward. But thou, when thou fastest, anoint thine head, and wash thy face; that thou appear not unto men to fast, but unto thy Father which is in secret: and thy Father, which seeth in secret, shall reward thee openly.**"* (Matt. 6:16-18 KJV).

Although, in the days of Jesus, fasting was mandatory in the Jewish culture once a year, most especially on the Day of Atonement (Lev.

23:32 KJV). History tells us that the Pharisees voluntarily fasted twice a week to impress the people with their "holiness."

The Lord wants us to depend on him through fasting just as Israel did in the wilderness. We read the experience of Israel in Deuteronomy 8:2-3 KJV, which the Lord Jesus also referred to:

"And thou shalt remember all the way which the LORD thy God led thee these forty years in the wilderness, to humble thee, and to prove thee, to know what was in thine heart, whether thou wouldest keep his commandments or no. And he humbled thee, and suffered thee to hunger, and fed thee with manna, which thou knewest not, neither did thy fathers know; that he might make thee know that man doth not live by bread only, but by every word that proceedeth out of the mouth of the LORD doth man live."

So, Jesus told them that it was not Moses who supplied the bread they ate, but *"...my Father who gives the true bread from heaven."* (Jn 6:32 KJV)

4. Fasting for healing

"Is not this the fast that I have chosen? To loose the bands of wickedness, to undo the heavy burdens, and to let the oppressed go free and that ye break every yoke? ....Then shall thy light break forth as the morning, and thine health shall spring forth speedily: and thy righteousness shall go before thee; the glory of the LORD shall be thy rereward." (Is. 58:6, 8 KJV)

If we understand the privilege we have in Christ Jesus, then we will take our infirmities, pain, and suffering to Jehovah Rapha *"...the Lord that healeth thee"* in prayer and fasting (Ex 15:26 KJV). And we would do it with the seriousness it demands. One of the salient principles we must trust and act on is the fact that we must not believe that the sickness we are going through can kill us. If we do otherwise, we have limited the power of God. Jesus said,

"This sickness is not unto death, but the glory of God, that the Son of God might be glorified thereby." (Jn. 11:4 KJV).

Seeking the face of God through prayer and fasting should be a lifestyle. Fasting carries tremendous power and provides us with medical therapy of healing for our bodies. For example, when the Lord through Isaiah told Hezekiah to put his house in order because he was going to die, Hezekiah did not agree with the verdict (Is. 38:1-2 KJV). He rejected the judgment instead of calling the family members to prepare his exit and organize his funeral arrangement he in fact challenged the verdict. He did not prepare for his death, but he cried unto the Lord to negotiate for length of days. We are told in verses 2 to 5 of that chapter that:

"Then Hezekiah turned his face toward the wall, and prayed unto the LORD, and said, Remember now, O LORD, I beseech thee, how I have walked before thee in truth and with a perfect heart, and have done that which is good in thy sight. And Hezekiah wept sore. Then came the word of the Lord to Isaiah, saying. Go, and say to Hezekiah, Thus saith the Lord, the God of David thy father, I have heard thy prayer, I have seen thy tears; behold I will add unto thy days fifteen years"

This scripture confirms to us that life is given; but long life must be negotiated. David in Psalm 21:4 KJV says about the king that: *"He asked life of thee, and thou gavest it him, even length of days for ever and ever."*

You must neither take the matter of length of days lightly, nor accept the verdict of premature death from the enemy, always pray for long life.

B. Guidelines for fasting:

1. Set your mind on the goal:

When you set your mind on the goal to approach God in fasting, you must be deliberate, focused, and intentional about it. Fasting for healing, direction, marriage and family, restoration or deliverance from financial difficulties or business ideas must be strategic and determined. For this reason, you would need to select relevant scriptures that you must stand on to deal with the areas of your need.

For example, if you are fasting for healing, select scriptures on healing, or those that directly address the matter. Let us, for example, review some healing scriptures together below:

"Who his own self bare our sins in his own body on the tree, that we, being dead to sins, should live unto righteousness: by whose stripes ye were healed." (1Pet. 2:24 KJV)

"For I will restore health unto thee, and I will heal thee of thy wounds, saith the LORD; because they called thee an Outcast, saying, This is Zion, whom no man seeketh after." (Jer. 30:17 KJV)

2. Other Related Life challenging Bible verses:

As Christians, we are bound to face challenges in life, but thanks be to God that we have the antidote in the word of God. God's word has life and light to deal with darkness (John 1:4-5 KJV). We are encouraged in the word of God to seek the truth of His word diligently and act on it. We see a good example in Isaiah 34:16 KJV: *"Seek ye out of the book of the LORD, and read: no one of these shall fail, none shall want her mate: for my mouth, it hath commanded, and his spirit hath gathered them."*

If you are going to see the hand of God when you fast and pray, you must practice addressing every circumstance through the effective use of the scripture.

Now that there is a global pandemic threatening lives, fear and anxiety have gripped the entire world. There is a possibility of sickness and disease making their impacts on those with pre-existing conditions. No matter what the illness may be, prayer and faith in the name of Jesus is the answer. You cannot afford to fear, He has promised to be with you.

"Fear thou not; for I am with thee: be not dismayed; for I am thy God: I will strengthen thee; yea, I will help thee; yea, I will uphold thee with the right hand of my righteousness." (Is. 41:10 KJV).

God bless you as you take time to deploy the weapons of prayer, fasting and the effective use of God's words to combat the challenging situations in your lives!

CHAPTER ELEVEN

THE MYSTERY OF THANKSGIVING AND PRAISE

Thanksgiving and Praise are mysteries that command triumph in men's lives. They are spiritual arsenals that when combined with prayer, they become dangerous weapons that are instrumental in fighting the powers of darkness. The Bible declares that:

"The weapons of our warfare are not physical [weapons of flesh and blood]. Our weapons are divinely powerful for the destruction of fortresses". (2 Cor. 10:4 KJV)

Therefore, as mortal human beings, we cannot use carnal weapons to fight the unseen forces of darkness. Instead, we must rationally choose which method will give us victory in this battle. Apostle Paul assures us that the mighty weapons suitable for this battle include prayer, faith in Christ Jesus, God's Word, the Holy Spirit, the Blood of Jesus, the name of Jesus etc. These and many others are the effective weapons that we must apply to break down Satanic power in our lives.

Thanksgiving and Praise are not rituals but mysteries of the kingdom of God and they are both like the parable the intellect cannot logically understand. Therefore, Thanksgiving and Praise are referred to as something outside the range of normal human activity and understanding that can only be comprehended through divine revelation and brought about by divine activity.

In 1st Samuel 2:1 KJV, Hannah praised the Lord who answered her petition for her son. Her prayer proved her confidence in God's sovereignty and her thankfulness for her blessings. The scripture recorded in verse 2 that Hannah praises God for being a rock, firm, strong, and unchanging.

"There is none holy as the LORD: for there is none beside thee: neither is there any rock like our God" (vs. 2 KJV)

In (Lk. 1:45-55 KJV), we also read that Mary, the mother of Jesus, modeled her thanksgiving and praise song, called the Magnificat, after Hannah's prayer. Like Hannah and Mary, believers should be confident in God's unfailing love who has ultimate control over every event in our lives.

A. The Mystery of Thanksgiving

Moses and Israelites crossed at the point of the heavy waves that parted the sea into two at the Red Sea, but when Pharaoh's army tried to do the same, they disappeared in the ocean waves. Thereafter, Moses and the sister Marian sang songs of victory.

"The LORD is my strength and song, And he is become my salvation: He is my God, and I will prepare him a habitation; My father's God, and I will exalt him." (Ex. 15:2 KJV).

My counsel here is that when something significant happens to you, you should show gratitude to God. Anyone who wants to enjoy victory tomorrow must thank God for what he has done for them today.

B. On what occasion should we be thankful to God?

1. When the future looks uncertain.

When Mary encountered her cousin Elizabeth for being pregnant out of wedlock, she could have condemned herself for this unexpected gift. Still, she glorified and rejoiced in the God of her salvation (Lk. 1:46-55 KJV). Mary was thankful to God with a song for what he would do to the world through her.

If you notice in these songs, God is seen as a champion of the poor, the oppressed, and the despised. *"From henceforth all the generations shall call me blessed."* (vs. 48 KJV). Does this mean that Mary was proud? No, she was recognizing, acknowledging, and accepting the gift of God. Pride is refusing to accept the gift or taking credit for what God has done to humanity.

2. When we face unseen battles

In 2nd Chronicles 20:20 KJV, the Bible tells us about Jehoshaphat, who faced three nations, Moabites, the Ammonites, and the Children of Mount Seir, who came against him to battle. He gathered the people, including their wives and children to come and praise the Lord. While they were at it, the Spirit of God came upon Jahaziel, a young man who announced to Jehoshaphat and Judah:

"...for the battle is not your's but God's.....Ye shall not need to fight in this battle: set yourselves, stand ye still, and see the salvation of the LORD with you, O Judah and Jerusalem: fear not, nor be dismayed; to morrow go out against them: for the LORD will be with you." (vs. 15, 17 KJV).

At this time, Jehoshaphat appointed singers to the frontlines of imminent war and used this song as their weapons.

"...Oh, give thanks unto the Lord, for His steadfast love endures forever. As they began to say, Praise the LORD; for his mercy endureth forever, THE Lord set an ambush against the Ammonites, Moab, and Mount Seir so that they began to attack each other." (2 Chron. 20:21-22 KJV)

Just thanking God sent total confusion into the camp of their enemies. Are you aware of the spiritual force of thanksgiving to God? It is capable of reverberating through the kingdom of darkness as thunder brings the enemy powers to naught. No wonder Paul the Apostle declares, the weapons of our warfare are not carnal (2 Cor. 10:4 KJV)

Like Paul, we do not need to use sophisticated weapons to win our battles, praise God! David declares with a shout of Triumph.

"Blessed be the Lord, my Rock and great strength, who trains my hands for war And my fingers for battle." (Ps. 144:1 KJV)

God made these weapons available for us to use as we engaged in this fight, but we must however decide what form or plans we like to make use of.

3. When the power of darkness batters us

"Because that, when they knew God, they glorified him not as God, neither were thankful; but became vain in their imagination, and their foolish heart was darkened." (Rom. 1:21 KJV).

They refused to ascribe the glory that belonged to Him nor speak honorably about Him as the creator of all things out of nothing. Their vain imagination and their darkened foolish hearts made them neither to glorify God nor be thankful. Lack of thanksgiving to God makes many suffer untold hardship.

C. Benefits of thanksgiving and Praise

1. Total wholeness.

One of the benefits of thanksgiving is enjoying total wholeness. For example, in Luke 17:17-19 KJV we read:

"And Jesus answering said, Where there not ten cleansed? but where are the nine? There are not found that returned to give glory to God, save this stranger. And he said unto him, Arise, go thy way: thy faith hath made thee whole."

The leper who came back to show gratitude to God was not just healed, he was made whole. Thanksgiving is the believer's victory amid what is impossible.

2. Multiplication and increase –

Thanksgiving and praise increase and multiply our resources *"..and I will multiply them, and they shall not be small."* (Jer. 30:19 KJV). It brings increases to churches, homes, and families. The Lord wants us to make thanksgiving our lifestyles because gratefulness is the gateway to open heaven. We read about the amazing power of thanksgiving in Mark 8:6-9 KJV. There, Jesus displayed the mystery of giving thanks to the multitudes who came to Him.

"Jesus replied, They do not need to go away,. You give them something to eat. Were the disciples perplexed with only five loaves of bread and two fish? Jesus took and lifted them up to the father in heaven and gave thanks to Him; just as the disciples began to share, they multiplied and had more than enough food to feed five thousand people with leftover baskets."

3. It **Releases the Presence of God**

Thanksgiving and Praise carry the Presence of God – the Bible tells us:

"When the children Israel were going out of Egypt the house of Jacob from a people of strange language; Judah became a sanctuary, And Israel His dominion. The Red Sea looked and fled; The Jordan turned back." (Ps. 114:1-3 AMP).

The sea and mountain trembled at His presence (thanksgiving and praise are the root meaning of the name Judah). Even with the technology of our days, the seas, rivers, and mountains still present us with formidable challenges. But to God, who controls nature, mountains and ocean are nothing before Him.

Thanksgiving is a mystery that releases God's glory. For example, in 2 Chronicles 5:13 KJV we read

"It came even to pass, as the trumpeters and singers were as one, to make one sound to be heard in praising and thanking the LORD; and when they lifted up their voice with the trumpets and cymbals and instruments of music, and praised the LORD, saying, For he is good; for his mercy endureth for ever: that then the house was filled with a cloud, even the house of the LORD." (2 Chron. 5:13 KJV).

Thus, the overflowing Praises provoked heaven; and there was an outpouring of His Presence in the house of the LORD. Therefore, thanksgiving and Praise are important components of our prayer.

". ...*but in everything by prayer and supplication with thanksgiving, let your requests be made known unto God.*" (Phil. 4:6 KJV).

Paul, the apostle, reminds us to combine all types of prayers with thanksgiving. These are immensely powerful and essential tools that also lead to peace (Col. 4:2 KJV).

Thanksgiving is the vehicle that transports our prayer to heaven 1st Thessalonians 5:16 reads: "*Rejoice always, pray continually, and give thanks in all circumstances, for this is God's will for you in Christ Jesus.*"

Even when we are not sure what the next thing will be or what is God's plan for our lives, a thankful, contented heart demonstrates trust in God's sovereignty and keeps the will of God at the center of his life.

In conclusion, as children of God, it is our responsibility to express our gratitude to God for what He has done in the past. We must thank Him for all that He is, and what He has given to us today and give thanks for the future fulfillment of His prophetic word in our lives. Gratitude to God is a spiritual force that empowers us to scale higher.

Grateful Christians enjoy supernatural powers from heaven that cause them to always work for Him, never run dry, and make fresh impacts.

CHAPTER TWELVE

THE PROPHETIC DECLARATION OF THE WORD

The Word of God is the most powerful weapon for believers. It is free, prosperous, great for healing and deliverance, protection and preservation, a veritable weapon in marriage, fruitfulness, anointing and spiritual empowerment, and finally, it gives direction and guidance. When the enemy strikes his arrow against you whether in the family, or your work setting you need to return the arrow back through the power of the Word of God. The Bible says the declaration of this powerful weapon against the enemy will stop the onslaught and cease further harassment:

"But what saith it? The Word is nigh thee, even in thy mouth, and in thy heart: that is, the Word of faith, which we preach." (Rom. 10:8 KJV).

And addition we are told in Isaiah 43:26: *"Put me in remembrance: let us plead together: declare thou, that thou mayest be justified."* (Is. 43:26 KJV). What does God mean when He says, *"Put me in remembrance"*? It means to remind me of my Word. In what way do you remind Him of what He has already said?

Search through His Word that addresses the issue in question and declare it in your prayer. In Paul's summary to the believers, he asserts that the Word of God is not merely a collection of words from the Bible. Neither is it a vehicle for communicating ideas; it is a living, life-changing, and dynamic in action when declared (Heb. 4:12 KJV). The quickest way to get God's attention is to constantly declare His word in your prayers.

A. Declaration of God's Word

Declare these verses of scriptures:

1. Healing

"*Who his own self bare our sins in His own body on the tree, that we, being dead to sins, should live unto righteousness: by whose stripes ye were healed.*" (1Pet. 2:24 KJV).

"*Behold, I will bring it health and cure, and l will cure them and will reveal unto them the abundance of peace and truth.*" (Jer. 33:6 KJV).

"*But he was wounded for our transgressions, he was bruised for our iniquities: the chastisement of our peace was upon him; and with his stripes we are healed.*" (Is. 53:5 KJV).

"*.. l am the LORD that health thee.*" (Ex. 15:26 KJV)

2. Deliverance.

"*Stand fast therefore in the liberty wherewith Christ hath made us free, and be not entangled again with the yoke of bondage.*" (Gal. 5:1 KJV)

"*Thou art my hiding place; thou shalt preserve me from trouble; thou shalt compass me about with songs of deliverance.*" (Ps. 32:7 KJV).

"*I sought the LORD, and he heard me and delivered me from all my fears. So they looked unto him, and were lightened: and their faces were not ashamed.*" (Ps. 34:4-5 KJV).

"For whatsoever is born of God overcometh the world: and this is the victory that overcometh the world, even our faith. Who is he that overcometh the world, but he that believeth that is the Son of God." (1Jn. 5:4-5 KJV)

3. Protection and Preservation

"The angel of the LORD encampeth round about them that fear him and delivereth them. O taste and see that the LORD is good: blessed is the man that trusteth in him. O fear the LORD, ye his saints: for there is no want to them that fear him." (Ps. 34:7-9 KJV)

"But the Lord is faithful, who shall stablish you and keep you from evil. And we have confidence in the Lord touching you, that ye both do and will do the things which we command. And the Lord direct your hearts into the love of God, and into the patient waiting for Christ." (2Thess. 3:3-5 KJV)

"No weapon that is formed against thee shall prosper, and every tongue that shall rise against thee in judgment thou shalt condemn. This is the heritage of the servants of the LORD, and their righteousness is of me, saith the LORD." (Is. 54:17 KJV).

"Keep me as the apple of thy eye, hide me under the shadow of thy wings, From the wicked that oppress me, from my deadly enemies, who compass me about." (Ps. 17:8-9 KJV).

"The LORD is my shepherd; I shall not want. He maketh me to lie down in green pastures: he leadeth me beside the still waters. He restoreth my soul: he leadeth me in the paths of righteousness for his name's sake. Yea, though l walk valley of the shadow of death, I will fear no evil: for thou art with me; thy rod and thy staff they comfort me." (Ps. 23:1-4 KJV)

B. Holy Spirit and Empowerment

"And he said unto me, My grace is sufficient for thee: for my strength is made perfect in weakness. Most gladly, therefore will

I rather glory in my infirmities, that the power of Christ may rest upon me." (2 Cor. 12:9 KJV).

"*Behold, I give unto you power to tread on serpents and scorpions, and overall the power of the enemy: and nothing shall by any means hurt you.*" (Lk. 10:19-20 KJV).

"*But the anointing which ye have received of him abideth in you, and need not that any man teach you: but as the same anointing teacheth you of all things, and is truth, and is no lie, and even as it hath taught you, ye shall abide in him.*" (1Jn. 2:27 KJV)

"*Then Samuel took the horn of oil, anointed him in the midst of his brethren, and anointed him in the midst of his brethren: and the Spirit of the LORD came upon David from that day forward. So Samuel rose up, and went to Ramah.*" (1Sam. 16:13 KJV).

In conclusion, declaring God's word is showing the fact that you trust Him to do what His word has promised. You are categorically stating that you are willing to stand in faith believing that His word will work in your situation. God's word can neither fail, nor be contradicted if deployed as a weapon in faith against any adversary. This is simply because: "*For ever, O Lord thy word is settled in heaven.*" (Ps. 119:89 KJV)

CHAPTER THIRTEEN

TESTIMONIES

A. Introduction

This chapter is dedicated to how the power of God manifested in answer to prayer amongst some of our brethren. Through resilient prayers till something happened they have been able to secure heavenly answers to their prayers. Securing answer to prayers is what this book is about, please find below their brief accounts of their personal testimonies.

1. A Son shall be Born as You Desire!

My testimony is on how the Lord used His servant, Pastor Anietie Affiah to open my eyes to the truth of God's word, in a unique way so much that it transformed my life. I have come to understand through his teachings that serving God pays and when I applied this knowledge received under his tutelage God answered.

It all began in 2007 when God spoke through him to tell me to apply Genesis 1 verse 27 KJV in my prayer, because at that time my wife and I were trusting God for a son after having had four (4) beautiful daughters. The text of that passage of the scriptures in part states "...*He created male and female*"

Like every father my desire was valid as I wanted them male and female. So, following his counsel, I did, and God also confirmed this verse of scripture to me in prayer on January 1st, 2008, after God graciously ushered us into the new year. On that day, during our "Feet Washing Service," Pastor Affiah washed our feet and declared that we should all go and bear fruits. Furthermore, God also gave me a word in Jeremiah 33 verse 17: KJV saying that "*...David will never lack a man to sit upon the throne...*". I received it with joy, in faith and expectation that God's settled word shall indeed be fulfilled in my family!

Beloved, that same January 2008 my wife took in, but the devil was not happy about it. However, God intervened again through Pastor Affiah in a vision, while I was with him in the church praying one midnight. In the vision he saw an old lady coming to my house, who saw a baby in the cot, and she picked up the baby, placed it on her on her back and left with it. In the vision, the Pastor who also was on his way to my house, was about to enter, when he saw the strange old lady with the baby on her back. He was sure she was not a member of my household, and so she asked her where she was taking the baby, but she ignored him and kept on going with the child. On a closer look he saw that the baby was a boy.

After our midnight prayer that night, I dozed off, so, he woke me up after the vision and instructed me that we should intensify our prayers because the enemy was planning to steal our joy. My wife and I intensified our prayers as he counseled and even slept in the church to pray after which God's servant came and blessed us the following day.

The baby began to grow and was nurtured by God without any incident till about October 2008 when the devil struck. My wife and her colleague were car-pooling, and as they left from work that day to go home, at about 11.45 pm, a city police officer who had no emergency light nor siren on drove about fifty-five miles in a twenty-five miles per hour zone and smashed into the car they were riding, totaling it. Even the baby in the womb flinched from the impact of the accident.

When my wife called to narrate the nature of the accident, she was in pain and shock, and I spoke to her as a son of a Prophet to calm down. I placed a call to Pastor Affiah and narrated the incident to him and he confirmed God's word that nothing would happen to the mother and child. As he decreed so it was, praise the Lord!

To the glory of God, two days after this accident, our son Onyebuchi Chiemeziem Eze was born, and he has grown so well in wisdom, knowledge, and stature to the point that he is now the drummer for the church at the age of twelve years old. I know the things of God are foolishness to the people of the world but not to my family and me. We have learnt a lot through our experience and have come to know that our God specializes in doing the impossibilities and what He promised He is able to do.

For this reason, I am grateful to God for using His Servant Pastor Anietie Affiah to be my father in the faith and a source of blessing. Glory be to God. Amen.

Elder Christ Eze

2. Hearing and Seeing Strong Faith in Action!

In the early Summer of 2010, I entered by chance the Discount Dry Cleaners outfit, and met one of the employees who was a long-lost family friend. During the chanced meeting we exchanged phone numbers and she invited me to visit her church Faith in Christ Church Worldwide (FICCW), but I had not heard of it until then. She gave me the address of the location which happened to be at a shopping mall, and I must say, I have not attended any church in a shopping mall before and would have never considered attending one. By my standard, a "real church" is a free-standing building with a minimum membership of 200 members.

However, I promised my family friend that I would attend later that Summer because I had a family, high school, and nursing school reunion celebrations to attend. Stemming from my deep desire to know the Lord, I had earlier thought of searching for a suitable place of worship here in Durham, but the question than was, "Which church?" In the past, I remembered attending a one-day presentation by a Duke Divinity professor on the New Testament which to me was unimpressive.

I also recall that when I was working at a substance abuse center, myself, and other nurses, as we interacted with the clients in their 12-step program, would call on the name of Jesus while counseling them. Still, Duke Divinity was never noted as using that name at all, and I knew I had to undertake the search for Jesus. For this reason, I decided to honor the promise I made to the family member, as a sign of honesty, to attend the church service at the shopping mall the last Sunday in August of 2010.

When I got to the church I expectedly sat next to my friend and thereby renewed my relationship. That Sunday, my word became my bond, and I thought I did my friend a favor by attending the church service at FICCW. During the service, I noticed that the congregation seemed friendly, and I could understand them clearly when they spoke to me for the most part.

At a point in the service, there was testimony time, and I realized that in the Baptist church I used to attend, we did not have testimony time. I was only aware of this being done only in the Holiness Church. The testifier was the Senior Pastor's wife, Pastor Colette Affiah. In her testimony she recounted the goodness of God and how He granted her a safe, uncomplicated delivery of a baby boy that she and Pastor believed Him for. She testified about her experience at the Great Duke University Hospital, America's fifth best Hospital during the birth of Jeremiah, their son. Before his birth she experienced premature labor but God, answered their prayers for safe delivery.

The background to this was that her water broke on her sixth month of pregnancy. In the process of her care, the doctor at Duke recommended a spinal tap on little Jeremiah because of a high white blood cell (WBC) count to determine further treatments. However, because of her unwavering faith in Christ, she decided that the doctor should first repeat the WBC count test before the spinal tap. She did and noted that the WBC count test had corrected so the spinal tap would no more be necessary. Then, with boldness in her spirit, she told the doctor in response that the God of Abraham, Isaac, and Jacob, in Jeremiah's life, had done it again as He promised. She furthermore declared to the doctor that her faith and that of her husband were founded upon the solid rock of Jesus Christ.

Up until this time, I had never witnessed a layperson exchange a seat of authority with a doctor based on faith! This was a revelation to me of the power of faith in Christ. I have heard of faith all my Christian life but had neither seen nor heard it in such a manner. It was at that moment that I realized what I was searching for, and I knew at that moment, **"That was exactly what I needed and had to have!"** At that instance, I knew I had to listen to God's word diligently and as a result, every time the church doors were opened, I was there.

Without any doubt, I knew that God sent me a Pastor as he said he would in Jeremiah 3 verse 15 KJV:

"and I will give you pastors according to mine heart, which shall feed you with knowledge and understanding."

A pastor who would teach me how to please my God. A pastor who God eventually used to reveal to me that my faith was in science and not in God. As Hebrew 11 verse 6 says:

"But without faith it is impossible to please him: for for he that cometh to God must believe that he is, and a rewarder of them that diligently seek him."

This in essence means that in all my years as a Christian, I had never pleased God; what a revelation! So, my God sent me a Pastor from Nigeria, in West Africa to ensure my name would be in God's book of life and that by His mercy I will prosper and be in health even as my soul prospers (Rev 20:15; 3 John 1:2 KJV).

I am so grateful to God for not only sending me a pastor but a church family. I am also thankful for the elders and co-workers in the vineyard that serve God with willing spirits. For example, in my conversation with one of the elders I was referring to all mankind as sinners, he corrected me in this teachable moment and said, no, Mother Val no, some of us are the redeemed of the Lord! We are not all sinners!

I see Pastor and his wife leading by example. It warms my heart to hear her refer to her husband as my Pastor, the man of God and gives accounts of numerous times she had sought his spiritual insight and prayers. She frequently honors him as the head of their family as designed by God. I see a hundred percent of the children and youth in the family unit with fathers and mothers, living and believing the word of God in this church to the glory of God.

It is only a Pastor sent by God that would unravel the mystery of God's word as he does day in and out. I am constantly experiencing the revelation of my Lord and Savior, and I am so pleased to be a member of the Faith in Christ Church Worldwide (FICCW), as I fondly say, **"The Church in the mall."** In conclusion, I thank God that this is my Bible college. Praise the Lord!

Mother Verital Robert

3. Jeremiah's Miraculous Delivery

The scripture in Psalms 127 verse 3 KJV says

"Lo, children are an heritage of the Lord: And the fruit of the womb is his reward."

Being fully aware of this promise given to us by Our God Almighty, in 2005, I sought for a son from the Lord in agreement with my husband. After our prayers the Lord blessed us with a male child, as I got pregnant that same year with Jeremiah, who by the grace of God is currently over fifteen years of age now. Initially, I had the normal changes that come with pregnancy but by God's infinite power and strength, I was still able to continue to do my schedule at the hospital where I work.

However, six months into the pregnancy, an unexpected problem occurred, and it only took the grace of God to overcome the shame the enemy tried to bring on my family and I. It is true and real that the scripture says in John 10 verse 10 KJV that the

"..thief came to steal, kill and destroy but that I have come that you may have life and have life more abundantly."

On that fateful morning, I woke up and as I tried to get out of the bed, I heard a sound from my stomach indicating that something just busted. As I looked to see what had transpired, an enormous amount of water (aka amniotic fluid) started gushing out of my body, and it flooded all around where I stood. I telephoned my husband who was at school at the time, and he immediately came back home. On arrival he prayed with me and thereafter rushed me to the then Durham Regional Hospital, now Duke Regional Hospital.

While we were enroute the hospital, my husband gave me a word:

"We will not lose our baby because the Lord has answered us with a miracle."

May I interject here, that in my twenty-two plus years of marriage to my husband, Senior Pastor Anietie Affiah, he will always say to me:

"Once we have prayed, let us not sit around and talk about the problem anymore. Let's just believe that the Lord has heard and answered us."

That has been the realm of operation we adopted in our marriage and family all these beautiful years we have been married to each other. As such, after my husband prayed for me, I was sure beyond all doubts that our baby was safe and secured in the arms of Jesus. After we arrived at the hospital, the doctor on duty checked me and after realizing what had occurred, informed me that he would have to transfer me from Durham Regional Hospital to Duke Hospital to enable me to receive a Level One medical care needed for my case.

It was like I was dreaming because I went from having a beautiful pregnancy journey to where I had to summon all my strength from God to believe that He would fight for me and my family. For God's Word came to me at that point from Exodus 14:14 KJV: that *"I will fight for you and you shall hold your peace."* and Psalm 46 verse 10

"Be still and know that I am your God….."

Additionally, I had to put on my mustard seed faith shoes to believe God wholly that no matter how the storm was raging, Jesus had already brought the calm more than two thousand years when He died for us on the cross of Calvary. It is a common knowledge that a child who is six months into pregnancy is not fully developed so having your water break when the baby is not fully developed can bring untold complications to the baby but for God. Ideally, a child should be in the womb till nine or ten months before the water usually breaks about few minutes into delivery.

There is the risk of serious infection to the baby's brain or spinal cord when the water is broken early in the pregnancy. Having this experience during six months of pregnancy while going into the seventh months, revealed to me it could only have been God who fought our battle and gave us the victory.

I was taken to Duke Hospital by my husband and as we arrived the nurses prepared us for emergent delivery, fearing that the baby would be born anytime on that day or before the week was out. At that time, I prayed to God that the baby should come only when Our God was ready for it to come and not according to the knowledge of man. I was admitted to the hospital because the doctors said that it was not safe for me or the baby to go back home. The plan was to put me on bedrest till the baby was born because every time I stood up water would flow out of me so uncontrollably. The doctors also wanted me to be in the hospital till the baby was born so that they could monitor it and ensure there was no signs of infection or other allied problems associated with this condition. During my hospitalization and period of waiting for the delivery of our son, my husband and I stood on Exodus 23 verse 26 KJV that says

"There shall nothing cast their young, nor be barren, in thy land…"

I knew that no matter what was happening, nothing on earth will cast my young because the word of the Lord said so. Proverbs 10 verse 22 KJV also says that *"The blessings of the Lord, it maketh rich, and added no sorrow with it."*

I understood through this scripture that since the Lord had blessed me with the fruit of the womb, no gate of darkness would prevail against the work of God in me, Halleluiah! I just knew it that the enemy had already been defeated, and the power of God had prevailed over the forces of the enemy. As a matter of fact, the knowledge was so strong that no matter what was happening, I knew victory had already been won for me and my family in the name of Jesus, Amen.

Every night, my husband (i.e., the man of God), and I prayed together breaking bread and drinking the blood of Jesus in holy communion to activate life on the baby because John 6 verse 56 KJV tells us to know:

"There is life in the eating of the flesh and the drinking the blood of Jesus."

Further to this, various vigorous tests which included daily ultrasound, lab draws, and fetal tones monitoring were conducted to ensure that the baby was in good condition. By the mercy of God Almighty, each day ultrasound was done, the level of water that remained in the womb was always enough to cushion the baby. The baby moved and grew well in the womb with no distress the whole of the time the amniotic fluid leaked out. The Lord took care of Jeremiah and made His power to abound in him mightily. The scripture says in Psalm 34:19 KJV that:

*"**Many are the afflictions of the righteous: But the Lord delivereth him out of them all**."*

The Lord truly delivered Jeremiah from untimely death and gave him back everything that the devil wanted to steal from him.

My husband prayed for me on September 21st, 2006, and this happened to be my eight months in pregnancy, and immediately after he left the hospital for his lectures, labor started, so I had to call him to inform him about this. He left the lecture room, returned to the hospital to meet me in extreme excruciating pain, and after three hours the Lord did his wondrous work and Jeremiah was born with no help from any doctor.

The Lord took the wheel completely and brought out Jeremiah singlehandedly whilst the doctors who waited for his arrival looked in amazement. He was born in the presence of over five doctors and many respiratory therapists because the medical doctors expected the worst to happen on, before or after delivery. Jeremiah Affiah, our baby was born on September 21st, 2006, and he was immediately taken to the Pediatric intensive care unit to be closely monitored.

At the intensive care unit, he was placed in the incubator with oxygen to help him breath and medications given through his vein. The doctor, thereafter, came to speak to me and my husband about the condition of our son. The Attending had a list of diagnoses on our son, and there were more than ten of these wrong with him. As the doctor was reading the list, and suddenly the power of God came upon me so great that I told her "Stop now!"

The doctor stopped reading the list and then I told her that those illnesses can never be the portion of my son. Later, the doctor told me that my son's white blood cell (WBC) count of 55 was the highest he had ever seen in Duke Hospital for a long time and that they wanted to do a lumbar puncture on him who by then was so tiny at four pounds eight ounces. I told the doctor that no lumbar puncture will be necessary but that if my son truly needed it, the Lord Almighty whom I serve would do the lumbar puncture tonight. The doctor asked me if I had another person in my family that speaks English apart from me because from the way I was speaking, it appeared I did not understand the magnitude of the problem. I told the doctor that I was speaking to her in English, and I asked her to continue to speak to me because I could understand her excellently well.

The doctor proceeded to say that the WBC count was too high that the lumbar puncture needed to be done and after that testing will be conducted with the sample of spinal cord fluid that would be drained from his brain to know what kind of antibiotics should be effective in the treatment of his infection. The doctor proceeded to say that the infection was in the brain and was emergent, that the lumbar puncture should be conducted as soon as possible, adding that the duration of the IV antibiotics would take at least six weeks to take effect. I asked the doctor where he would like the WBC to drop to and the doctor answered that it would be better if it dropped from 55 to 4. In response I told he r that she should draw his blood the following day at 6.00am and check it, he would see that the WBC had dropped from 55 to 4.

My husband anointed the baby in the incubator with oil and prayed for him. We now went back to my hospital room that I had been in for over a month to continue to stand on God's word. We prayed that the Lord would wage war against the kingdom of the enemy. The following day, the doctor told us that they needed a consent to place a nasogastric tube so that the baby could be fed through the tube. I told the doctor that since Jesus did not eat through a tube, my baby would eat the normal way. I told the doctor that I would bring breast milk to the nurse later in the day to feed my son.

Later, I took my breast milk to the intensive care unit to be given to him and I returned later in the day and was told by the nurse that our son's strength was too high that he collapsed the nipple of a preemie child, that of a one to three months nipple but was able to eat with a bigger nipple of three to six months baby.

Furthermore, the nurse said that there was an angelic presence around our child that she could not explain which she said was so glorious. Then the Attending for the Duke Children's hospital called me to her office to ask me what kind of a person I was that no matter what they saw in my son never occurred. She wanted to know the difference between me and the other patients that when they were told that something was wrong with their children, they saw the problem occur in them. However, she said that with my case it was not so that I always told them my son was alright and that nothing was wrong with him only to see that it always turned out the way I said it would be.

In my response, I told her that we had carefully invested in the kingdom of heaven and that when she told us so and so was wrong with our son, all we did was to go to heaven and acquire needed spare parts in prayer for him.

Furthermore, I told her we did not merely just have the baby from being pregnant but just as Hannah sought the Lord for Samuel so also, I sought the Lord for him. I told her that I was convinced that the God whom I served who gave Samuel to Hannah would see to it that the baby would be completely healthy from the crown of his head to the sole of his feet.

The good news was that the baby got well and after less than two weeks, he was discharged from the hospital. The Lord Almighty has continued to show Himself strong in Jeremiah's life. The doctor said that he would not be able to walk on his legs, breathe without oxygen machine or eat without a feeding tube but by the grace and power of God our son excels in performance and strength for our God who continues to flow in him richly.

To God be the glory for the great things He had done and continues to do in Jeremiah's life. For truly, God has given us in Jeremiah, the double blessing for every shame the enemy wanted to bring to us. May God's name and power continue to reign forever and ever in the name of Jesus, Amen.

Colette Affiah

COMMENDATIONS

Indeed, many books on prayer have been written and many more will still be. But this book "The Prayers that Secure Heavenly Answer" is unique, in the sense that it is written, not just from an academic perspective, but experiential. Prayer is an invocation or an act that seeks to activate a rapport, in the case of Christians, with God Almighty. As I read the book from cover to cover, I found it to be insightful and inspirational, and it speaks to every area of a believer's prayer life. I certainly was personally blessed, and I just thank God for using His vessel, Pastor Affiah to produce such a masterpiece.

It is a book that I will recommend as a must-read for all those that are desirous of a deeper knowledge of the theology of prayer and its potency. I find the book to be fundamental to developing a holistic approach to a result-oriented prayer life. I commend the author for the simplicity of the presentation and the depth of knowledge of the subject. More Grace.

Ola R. Oyegunwa
Snr. Pastor
Divine Revelation International Church of Christ (DRICC)

The Author, Pastor Aniete Affiah, writes with strong convictions, and has been very careful to back up his points with Scriptures, emphasizing the power of the word of God and the need to stand on what the word says when we pray. This is very important, since, if we expect God to answer our prayer, we must pray according to His will as stated in Scriptures.

He also clearly states the conditions for effective prayer. In many instances, he has also used natural phenomena very effectively to illustrate Spiritual events, so that the reader can understand with clarity the message of the Scriptural events, and know how to apply the lessons therein.

The book ends with very powerful personal testimonies given by members of his Church, including his wife, who have applied the Bible based principles emphasized by the author, and have obtained positive results, to the Glory of God. The book attests to God's Faithfulness and willingness to answer our prayer when we pray according to God's will, as stated in the Scriptures.

Book Reviewer:
by Dr. Simon Ugwuoke
July 31, 2022

It was the great man of prayer E. M. Bounds, who wrote that:
"What the Church needs to-day is not more machinery or better, not new organizations or more and novel methods, but men whom the Holy Ghost can use - men of prayer, men mighty in prayer. The Holy Ghost does not flow through methods, but through men. He does not come on machinery, but on men. He does not anoint plans, but men -- men of prayer."

The above quote evidences, the life of Pastor Anietie Affiah, and the men and women he's been entrusted with. God's method for advancing his plans and purposes in our world is through men, men of prayer. You cannot lead people to where you have not been. God needed a man who has passed through the rigors of the desert (wilderness) to lead Israel to the promised land and chose Moses.

Pastor Affiah, is a man steeped in the power of prevailing prayer, and he has been endowed with the gift of leading a generation of people of prayer in advancing God's agenda for the current and future generations. This book imparts and gives unto readers, pertinent prayer keys needed to triumph over life's issues. This book contains not only theoretical prayer narratives, but the practical biblical applications to solving many life's salient issues, that help to build faith in God. He carefully lays down practical approaches and benefits of prayer. His many testimonies to me bears witness.

The word of the Lord in Proverbs 4:7 says,

*"**Wisdom is the principal thing; therefore get wisdom: and with all thy getting get understanding.**"*

Pastor Anietie has given us the how, why and when to pray, enunciating praying the revealed Word of God to continuously triumph over life's issues in the secret place of prayer.

Finally, the great Charles Spurgeon said,

"To pray is to enter the treasure-house of God and to gather riches out of an inexhaustible storehouse."

That is what this book has given its readers, and I am glad to recommend this book.

T. Peter Oke-Bello, CPA, D. Min.
Presiding Apostle,
King's Delight Global Ministries
Raleigh, North Carolina.

Printed in the United States
by Baker & Taylor Publisher Services